The 12-Month Gardener

The 12-Month Gardener

Simple Strategies for Extending Your Growing Season

Jeff Ashton

LARK BOOKS

A Division of Sterling Publishing Co., Inc.
New York

For the nights I went to bed too early, and left before they were awake; for their patience while I wrote this book, I dedicate this endeavor to my wife and kids, Eleanor, Jasmine, and Laurel

Editor: Joe Rhatigan
Art director: Celia Naranjo
Editorial assistance: Rain Newcomb
Production assistance: Hannes Charen, Theresa Gwynn
Illustrations: Olivier Rollin
Cover Photography: Sandra Stambaugh, also photographs on pages 2, 6, and 61

Library of Congress Cataloging-in-Publication Data

Ashton, Jeff, 1954–
    The 12-month gardener : simple strategies for extending your growing season / Jeff Ashton.
        p. cm.
    ISBN 1-57990-193-x
        1. Vegetable gardening. 2. Gardening 3. Vegetable gardening—Calendars.
    4. Gardening —Calendars. I. Title: Twelve month gardener. II. Title.
    SB321 .A84 2001
    635'.048--dc21

                                        2001029406

10 9 8 7 6 5 4 3 2 1
First Edition

Published by Lark Books, a division of
Sterling Publishing Co., Inc.
387 Park Avenue South
New York, N.Y. 10016

Distributed in Canada by Sterling Publishing,
c/o Canadian Manda Group, One Atlantic Ave., Suite 105
Toronto, Ontario, Canada M6K 3E7

Distributed in Australia by Capricorn Link (Australia) Pty Ltd.,
P.O. Box 704, Windsor, NSW 2756, Australia

Distributed in the U.K. by Guild of Master Craftsman Publications Ltd.,
Castle Place 166 High Street, Lewes, East Sussex, England, BN7 1XU
Tel: (+44) 1273 477374 • Fax: (+44) 1273 478606
Email: pubs@thegmcgroup.com • Web: www.gmcpublications.com

If you have questions or comments about this book, please contact:
Lark Books
50 College Street
Asheville, North Carolina 28801
(828) 253-0467

Manufactured in Hong Kong by Dai Nippon Printing, Ltd.

ISBN 1-57990-193-x

Contents

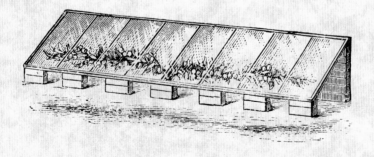

Introduction

A COUPLE OF YEARS AGO, my gardening pal Maurie McClure called me up, bemoaning the fact that frost was just around the corner and her gardening season would soon draw to a close. Now, this is a woman who has lived and breathed warm-weather gardening for years: she aggressively conserves water in times of drought to make sure her garden doesn't suffer, and unlike me, she even knows the Latin names of most of the plants in her garden. She's an honest-to-goodness, hard-core gardener; however, she had never extended her gardening season before. Season extension means just that— you're extending the length of the season that plants can grow in your garden. It's gardening that continues in spite of frosts that will normally kill half the plants in a typical summer garden.

I told Maurie she really didn't have to give it up when cold weather set in. I explained to her how she could set up a simple contraption, called a row cover, for extending her season. She seemed slightly uncertain and vaguely intimidated by the mysteries of season extension. She said her husband, David, was too busy to put one up. I told Maurie she could do it herself.

As it turns out, she did as I suggested. She went to the local garden center and picked up the last six packs of lettuce, kale, bok choy, parsley, and kohlrabi. She also bought spinach and radish seeds and planted them all in one 4 x 8-foot (1.2 x 2.4 m) bed. At the same garden center, she bought a package of season extension fabric called floating row cover that is *de rigueur* for hardy gardening enthusiasts. Maurie then went to the local home improvement center and picked up the parts she needed to make the wire ribs of a miniature, Quonset-style greenhouse to protect her newly planted, early fall garden.

Three weeks later, after the first hard frosts of fall, Maurie called me back squeaking with excitement over the progress of the plantings under the protection of the tunnel. "If I had known how simple this season extension business is, I would have started doing it long ago. When I lay the fabric down each

night, I get the same feeling I had when I tucked my son into bed when he was a baby!"

The truth is, there are plenty of reasons to get excited about cool-weather gardening: there are fewer insect pests, weeds are easier to control, and cold-hardy greens are sweeter and happier.

Maurie's approach was a sensible one. It drew on her experience as a warm-weather gardener and embraced ideas new to her about ways to make the gardening season continue longer. With a little bit of gardening experience under your belt, you can do the same thing. There's no mystery involved in season extension; plants have no hidden agenda to stop growing in cold weather. They only require a little love that you can give them and the protection of season extension contraptions that you'll learn to put together by reading this book.

Now, before you start thinking, "This sounds great, but who has the time?" my wife and I both have jobs and share a hectic schedule of community involvement, kids' activities, and domestic responsibilities. However, in spite of our busy lifestyles, we grow food in the garden year-round. And we do it in the cold months using season extenders of different sorts that are pretty darn simple to put together. So can you.

You'll get a rush knowing that your garden is still growing while your less-assertive gardening neighbors have already abandoned their vegetable plots for the winter. And, you'll be pleased to know that you don't need to be a master gardener or expert carpenter to get started. All it takes is the desire to keep on gardening!

Getting Started

T HE TERM "SEASON EXTENSION" needs to be defined. It's pretty simple, and it has four elements that correspond to the seasons:

⚜ In the spring, it means you've started plants out in the garden and have protected them in some manner before the last frosts of winter have gone away.

⚜ In the summer, it means you've kept cold-hardy plants from bolting by protecting them from the heat.

⚜ In the fall, it means you've protected summer-started crops so they continue to live and grow (at a slower rate) after frosts arrive, extending your harvest.

⚜ In the winter, it means you've planted and protected crops that are growing and thriving in spite of repeated frosts and cold weather.

All four can be achieved simply and effectively with the help of different kinds of contraptions that are surprisingly easy to put together, one or more of which will most likely be the perfect fit for your garden, your plants, your available time, and your wallet.

Now, my use of the word "protected" is a bit strong and suggests that you can keep plants covered as you would a bubble child. Your plants don't need or desire isolation from the outside. Though I'll be using the word "protect," I want to convey that season extension is a way to enhance the growing environment. The main way to do this is to cover individual plants, beds, rows, or whole gardens with traditional contraptions. However, season extension also means looking at your garden from a broader perspective, which may invite using nontraditional materials and techniques when the need arises.

Frost has arrived, and midsummer-planted greens enjoy the protection of a row cover.

Opening My Eyes

The first time I really extended my gardening season was an accident. I had planted an end-of-summer crop of spinach too late in the year. The plants grew about 2 inches (5.1 cm) and then went dormant because of an early winter. I bemoaned my procrastination that resulted in a crop getting stopped in its tracks before maturity, and assumed it would die out during the approaching Zone-5 winter. I forgot about the late-planted spinach until the following early spring when I noticed a patch of green in the garden. It turned out that the spinach had experienced a growth spurt during an unseasonably warm period. Without so much as the courtesy of a covering of straw, the spinach had survived snow, ice, and temperatures as low as -7°F (-22°C), and had come back as one of the tastiest spinach crops I've ever produced in my garden.

That spinach patch had gone through a process called *overwintering*. It's a gardening strategy that's been in use for at least 200 years, and it's the easiest way to get a really early crop of cold-hardy veggies in the spring. The process is simple. Sow seeds in the fall about three weeks before frosts are expected. The seedlings emerge and begin growing, but they stop when the hard cold sets in. At that point, a light screen of scattered straw will give the seedlings enough protection to take the edge off wind damage. In the spring, they start growing when Mother Nature says it's time.

Harvesting a crop from my garden before I had even planted other crops made a major impact on me and was a defining moment in my understanding of the possibilities in the garden. For years, I had skimmed over articles in magazines about cold frames. I understood what they were, but I never really considered putting one together. The occasional charts I found showing latitudes and suggested angles of the top (to maximize sun penetration) seemed confusing. I simply assumed the first frost of the season meant the end of all gardening for me. But that overwintered patch of spinach opened my eyes. I said to myself, "Buckaroo, if you can grow an early crop of spinach this good by pure luck, what could you do if you put some energy into figuring things out a bit?"

This book is the result of the energy I put into figuring out the many ways that one could extend the garden season. Along with detailed instructions for creating your own season extenders, this book also includes strategies that don't necessarily include using contraptions, as well as a closer look at cold-hardy plants (plants that prefer to grow in cold weather and can survive some pretty nasty weather).

Season Extension Contraptions

The next several chapters will explore ways to make and use cloches, cold frames, and greenhouses—all used for hundreds of years. We'll also look at more recently developed devices, such as tunnels and fabrics, which are commonly used by gardeners and farmers.

WHICH DEVICES ARE RIGHT FOR YOU?

It isn't necessary to make a permanent installation of a cold frame if you desire the flexibility of tunnels. And you don't need a garden greenhouse to be able to grow vegetables out of season. Each offers its own excellent advantages when used by themselves or when used together. It's important to evaluate what you want to achieve by extending the season, and then choose ones that make sense.

Farm-scale use of fabric to start salad greens

FABRICS

Season extension fabrics are spun-bonded, gauze-like materials that are new on the scene of climate modification in the garden. They're fabulous for starting seeds in beds, and they're essential for creating the simplest and most cost-effective enhanced growing environments.

PVC pipe hoops spanning a bed of broccoli, covered with 6-mil, construction-grade plastic

TUNNELS

Tunnels are relatively inexpensive ribs placed over a garden bed or row, which are then covered by a season extension fabric or plastic. Their length can easily be stretched to cover as long a 4-foot-wide (1.2 m) growing area as you desire. Tunnels are effective for covering full beds of salad greens, and they have the headroom to grow tall kale and mustards as well.

Plastic-covered stoop house spanning three garden beds

STOOP HOUSES

Stoop houses offer the advantage of covering a 12-foot-wide (3.6 m) area of garden beds that you can enter to work and harvest from. They're usually set up in the fall to cover existing beds and are taken down the following spring. They're Spartan-like structures that are flexible and inexpensive, and they create terrific microclimates. In the summer, they allow folks in colder climates to grow melons, cucumbers, tomatoes and other warm-weather crops.

CLOCHES

Cloches have been around 400 years and were originally made of glass in the shape of a bell that measured 16 to 18 inches (40.6 to 45.7 cm) in diameter. Contemporary, commercially manufactured cloches are made of plastic or waxed paper, while homemade cloches can be something as simple as a 1-gallon (3.8 L) plastic juice bottle with the bottom cut out. Regardless of the material from which they're made, all cloches are about the same size as the old-time bell jars, and remind me of miniature greenhouses sitting in the garden. Cloches are very effective for starting seeds and protecting individual plants. They're easy to move around and store.

Late 19th century market gardeners tending to glass cloches

Home-made cloches protecting tomatoes and pepper seedlings before the threat of frost has passed

COLD FRAMES

Cold frames can be permanent or semipermanent contraptions that are essentially a bottomless box with a transparent top. They allow you to grow salad greens, develop transplant stock from seed, and force bulbs. They're great for hardening off plants that have been grown indoors, and they're your best investment for a long-term contraption that will fill all your season extension needs.

Cold frame in vented position

GARDEN GREENHOUSE

Greenhouses are permanent installations that allow you to use the same structure year after year and gradually improve your ability to produce food throughout the winter. They're big enough to grow a significant amount of food, and they allow for greater use of insulation, as well as rock or water for heat storage. In addition, greenhouses allow you to easily cover crops inside with other layers to protect them during periods of extreme cold.

14 x 20 (4.2 x 6 m) greenhouse covering three raised beds

A Philosophy to Live By

Given the will, commitment, and resources to do so, you can grow anything you want through the winter. However, my philosophy is that it's so much easier to assist nature than it is to control it. That, along with my hectic schedule, is why my advice in this book is based on the following:

§ My garden must deliver the most food throughout the year with the least amount of work.

§ In warm weather, I focus on warm-weather crops, and I extend the season as much as an extra five weeks a year into the fall using fabrics and contraptions to produce significantly greater harvests.

§ In the winter, I grow cold-hardy crops that thrive in cold weather in the enhanced growing environment of contraptions.

§ I don't try to produce cold-hardy crops for my table in the heat of the summer, and I don't try to produce warm-weather crops in the winter. To be perfectly frank, by the time the first real killer freeze of the fall takes summer crops, I'm happy to see them go, because it finally means the end to the processing of harvested crops for storage that's a part of late-summer gardening. If you speak to gardeners who produce food year-round, you'll hear the same sentiments because it's the natural progression of year-round gardening.

A Few Words about Gardening Zones

Kale, broccoli, lettuce, arugula, and other various greens grown under multiple coverings

Possibly the most innovative organic market gardener in the western world today is Eliot Coleman, who grows greens and root crops for market from October to May in Zone 4/5 coastal Maine. To cope with harsh winters, he grows crops in raised beds covered with fabric, which are then covered with a tunnel. The multiple, twice-covered rows of crops are also covered by a complete greenhouse. Coleman maintains that each successive layer over a crop has the climate modification value of moving the garden one-and-a-half gardening zones to the south. In effect, Coleman's crops are growing in conditions found in Georgia at the same time of year.

There's no question that some folks in gardening Zone 4 use season extension contraptions to grow food well after the first frost of fall, and much before the last frosts of spring. Folks in Zone 5 can do that, plus they can achieve cold-hardy crop production if they put together systems such as those found in this book. And folks like me, who live on the cusp of Zone 5 and 6, can grow food very effectively in contraptions throughout the winter. For gardeners who live in Zone 7, winter is the only time they can grow some cold-hardy crops, and season extension contraptions will give an early opportunity to plant warm-weather crops before the heat of midsummer makes gardening a withering experience.

All contraptions can be used in all zones; the issue here isn't what zone is the best zone for a specific contraption, so much as what contraption is the best one for what you want to accomplish.

Preparing for the Inevitable

With the exception of my wife's birthday and our anniversary, the most important dates I've committed to memory are the first and last recorded frost dates for my garden. Your local government gardening offices can tell you the first and last average frost dates for your area, but your best source is to ask old-time gardeners or commercial greenhouse operators who live nearby. Chances are pretty good they know exactly when their earliest fall frost has occurred. For example, the average date of first fall frost, according to my cooperative extension office, is October 20. My neighbor Alan Salmon tells me, however, that the earliest frost he's ever experienced here in our valley occurred October 6. So that's my date for being ready. Even if Mother Nature is lenient, I know I'll still get frost by October 25. While on the subject of frost, it's worth noting that the temperatures heard on the radio are usually recorded at the airport. Those temperatures are taken 25 miles (40 km) from my house, and at a considerably lower elevation. Readings are also taken 5 feet (1.5 m) off the ground. Ground level vegetable gardens will be colder than temperatures would indicate because cold air drops to the lowest point. That's enough difference for me to know that locally reported temperatures are more an indication of general trends than a reliable source of readings for my particular garden. A better indication of impending frost in my garden is a general frost alert, a "nip in the air," and clear evening skies (which result in quick radiational cooling of the ground).

A New View of Failure

When folks think about season extension, the first thing that often comes to mind is an image of plastic structures set up in the garden in the late spring to protect newly planted tomato plants. There are some folks who utilize this strategy year after year, and certainly this is a part of season extension. But limiting your view of season extension to a relatively short span of time at one part of the year is like driving around in first gear. There's a wonderful potential for

continued garden activity as weather changes. All you need to do is shift gears with a new, year-round way of thinking.

As I've stated, part of this new gardening paradigm is gaining a fundamental understanding of various season extension contraptions and how they can be used effectively. But a gardener's greatest ally is the ability to anticipate the different needs of plants growing in the frost-filled portions of the year. And that comes only by getting out there and doing it. As you experiment with season extension, you'll inevitably lose plants because of freezing. This isn't failure. If you don't lose plants occasionally, it indicates you're not taking enough risks. Embrace your failure as a personal learning curve. Seeds are cheap, and success is the promise of great veggies from your garden while the neighbors are eating supermarket produce. As you become more proficient in the use of season extension contraptions, you'll be pushing the envelope and planting earlier and earlier.

If You Don't Do Anything Else

What I'd like this book to do is help you expand your horizons in the garden. Think of this as a roadmap to help you lengthen your gardening season through climate modification. After reading this book, if nothing else, you'll learn how to grow excellent salad greens under fabric or tunnels. But, I also hope you'll come away from this experience with a broader understanding of what it means, not only to garden in the winter, but also, how to optimize your time and your harvests through observation and experimentation.

An early winter view of Oriental greens, lettuce, and arugula

Materials, Tools, and Construction Hints

'M ALWAYS ON THE LOOKOUT for something useful that someone else has thrown away. Half the raised beds in my garden have wooden sides made of discarded redwood that came from a demolished deck. My manure tea barrel is a 45-gallon (171 L) juice drum that was given to me because I was in the right place at the right time. I mention this because there are plenty of opportunities to obtain free and/or cheap recycled materials for your garden contraptions that work just as well as newly purchased items. So when I have a good recycled material you can use, I mention it.

Recycled, old-fashioned cypress cold frame sashes, half covered in plastic, protecting the plants inside a mortared-stone cold frame

Covers

It's a given that the covers in this section help create enhanced growing environments for your plants, but there aren't enough similarities between them to say that a season extension material should do one certain thing. The coverings detailed here have different functions and allow different things to happen. All covers keep the cold out to varying degrees, and they all let light in. Plastic covers keep water out as well, and fabrics allow moisture in.

Glass

As I will again talk about in No-Pain Cold Frames (see page 60), the use of glass in the garden presents a definite danger to pets and kids who, at some point, will climb on top of a cold frame, or kick through some other home-

Though glass was used extensively for garden extension for hundreds of years, there are many safer and more effective materials available today.

spun glass contraption. Apparently, the allure of a raised platform of a cold frame in the middle of a garden is too much to resist. I've spoken with many experienced gardeners who have used old-fashioned cold frames with glass sashes for many years, and I've heard horror stories from at least half of them of kids, animals, or adults who were cut because they fell onto the frame, climbed on top and broke through, or sat on the frame thinking the glass would hold their weight. For hundreds of years, glass was the ideal material for extending the season in the garden, but there are numerous choices that give modern gardeners a broader base of options.

WINDOW SASHES

Though I don't recommend glass, I heartily recommend using window sashes that are the appropriate size for making cold frames, vent frames, or tepee cloches. Old-fashioned storm window frames with the glass removed are per-

Traditional storm windows with plastic covering a poured-cement cold frame that was built in the 1940s

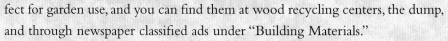

fect for garden use, and you can find them at wood recycling centers, the dump, and through newspaper classified ads under "Building Materials."

It's especially important to use caution when removing the glass from vintage windows because they'll usually shatter into dangerous pieces. To break the glass safely, lay the window down on a tarp. With your safety glasses on, start tapping on the glass with a hammer. Once the glass starts to break up, reduce all pieces to 3 inches (7.6 cm) in size or smaller and use the tarp to collect the pieces and funnel them into an appropriate container for proper disposal.

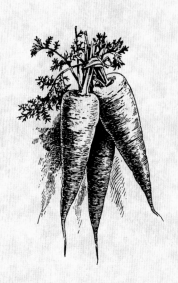

Sashes sans the glass sometimes lose structural integrity, but that can be remedied by securing corners and joints with framing plates (see page 26). Also, some sashes may be coated with lead-based paint. It's a good idea to apply two coats of quick-dry latex primer to seal in any possible lead paint (it also makes the sashes look good).

RIGID PLASTIC

One of the best finds I made at the local dump was a dozen sheets of 40 x 72-inch (1 x 1.8 m) clear, rigid plastic. I don't know what the original use for these panels was, but I covered four different cold frame sashes with the material by predrilling holes with a $^1/_8$-inch (3 mm) bit and attaching them with pan-head screws. One of my own sashes that I covered with this material had to be replaced after several years because the plastic clouded over—a common occurrence with plastics not intended for greenhouses. There are rigid greenhouse plastics that have long life expectancies and don't cloud up as quickly, and I've been very satisfied with the performance of a couple different greenhouse plastics that are on the market. Though you can purchase rigid plastics (which are treated to prevent clouding and cracking) from greenhouse supply catalogs, the same material is sometimes available at lumberyards. When you find a possible material, ask to see a "spec sheet" on file at the place of business to determine whether it's appropriate for intense sun and cold conditions. You'll need a jigsaw with a fine blade to cut these materials, although metal shears work great on some of the thinner acrylics if you have burly enough hands to make the cuts. Although a screw will go right through these rigid plastics, predrilling is

A rigid plastic sash protects cold-hardy plants from the snow.

Corrugated plastic covering a sunken cold frame filled with potted perennials

necessary or else you'll find that occasional cracks will unexpectedly race across the surface of your new plastic panel when you drive in the screws.

CORRUGATED GREENHOUSE PANELS

I have seen cold frame sash coverings made of a corrugated plastic greenhouse material that's available at home centers and is manufactured to resist clouding. They're very reasonably priced and are carried as a stock item in most lumberyards and home centers. You can buy strips of wood to fill the corrugated voids when a panel is attached to a cold frame. One gardener I know left these voids open at intervals on the topside of the sash to facilitate the venting of hot air that accumulates. You can expect good performance from corrugated greenhouse plastic on cold frame sashes, but after three or four seasons of cold-weather use, they'll start to crack and break up because of the constant opening and closing of the cold frame. This material also bends easily down its length to create a great cloche. It will last five or six years before breaking down from UV damage.

6-MIL CONSTRUCTION-GRADE POLYURETHANE PLASTIC

6-mil plastic covering a tall cold frame. Photo by Sue Waterman

Construction-grade polyurethane plastic sheeting is very cost-effective, although you usually have to buy it in 100-foot (30 m) rolls. This material can be found in the lighter grade 4-mil, but the heavier 6-mil isn't that much more expensive, and it's worth it for the extra bulk. Alas, the plastic won't last more than a year because it becomes brittle due to ultraviolet radiation and will eventually shatter and scatter little pieces of plastic all across your garden. Six-mil plastic is cheap enough that I keep a 20 x 100-foot (6 x 30 m) roll in my garden shed as a sort of insurance policy. I always have it there so I can cut off pieces when I need something quick to cover plants threatened by a cold snap. If you buy a roll and keep it in the box, you'll have an excellent source of material for emergencies. It's the perfect material for covering a stoop house.

Six-mil plastic is also a common and very popular covering for tunnels; a 10-foot-wide (3 m) roll is the perfect size if you're spanning a 3- to 4-foot-wide (.9 to 1.2 m) bed. If you don't mind changing the plastic each winter, you can also use it to cover cold frame sashes. During one bitter winter, when sixteen major ice storms hit southern New England (where I was living at the time), I had the opportunity to see the durability of this material. I had restored a 60-foot-long (18 m) vintage cold frame and enclosed the sashes with various coverings to observe their performance. One of the many sashes was covered with one layer of 6-mil plastic. Another was wrapped twice with the same material, and another was wrapped with three layers. The fourth ice storm destroyed the plastic on the sash with the single layer, while the other two survived the entire winter intact.

Another product that's becoming more readily available at garden centers is a 4-mil polyurethane plastic with precut slots to facilitate venting when the material's used as a tunnel. Venting tunnels is especially important when the tunnels are more than 15 feet (4.5 m) long because of the heat buildup at the center of the contraption.

GREENHOUSE PLASTIC FILMS

Look in any greenhouse supply catalog and you'll find several different clear, flexible coverings used in hoop-style greenhouses. These coverings look just like the 6-mil construction-grade plastic, but they are better suited for garden use. If you're ordering plastic by mail, it doesn't make sense to purchase a two-year plastic when a four-year plastic is only slightly more expensive. Four-year greenhouse plastics are UV-resistant, and you can find some that have special additives that reduce condensation. One challenge the home gardener will find in purchasing these plastics for covering a small greenhouse is that most greenhouse companies require that you buy a full 100-foot (30 m) roll. Shipping alone can be prohibitive unless you share the cost with one or two other practical gardeners who also wish to build greenhouses. If you ask around and call people who operate greenhouses, you can sometimes get a piece the size you need for a greenhouse, although most commercial greenhouses are sized to not leave much scrap from a roll of greenhouse film. Scraps from greenhouses may be large enough to cover cold frame sashes. Four-mil plastic allows significantly more light in than 6-mil, and it's nearly as durable if it's stretched and attached properly.

There are opportunities to find used greenhouse plastic for free. As a matter of course, many commercial greenhouse operators change the coverings every three years, even though the coverings are usually rated for a four-year life expectancy. Early retirement for a greenhouse covering is common because it provides insurance against the chance a greenhouse covering will self-destruct from UV-radiation stress and high winds, and expose valuable plants to the elements. You'd be surprised how many used greenhouse coverings find an early grave. Quite often you can get another couple of years out of such a covering if you can be there when the coverings are changed. The easiest way to be at the right place at the right time is to volunteer to help cover a commercial greenhouse when the change will be made. Big greenhouses take a fair number of people to hold edges that are flapping in the wind as new coverings are being installed, and many commercial greenhouse owners will take you at your word and call for the volunteer effort.

This 4 x 12-foot (1.2 x 3.6 m) frame is insulated with rigid insulation to a depth of 16 inches (40.6 cm). The seedlings in the frame will be transplanted into the garden later in the spring.

Nylon-Reinforced, UV-Resistant Plastic

For more northerly locations, gardeners use 8- to 12-mil, nylon-reinforced, UV-resistant plastic. Years ago, I used this material to raise the sides of a cold frame by covering panels that were made using the bent framing plates described on page 26. I found that nylon-reinforced plastic cut back on the amount of light that came into the frame, and it lasted eight years before it began to become brittle and yellow. You can also sew this material, which offers a lot of possibilities for creating extra cold-weather covers for your cold frame while still allowing light in.

Painter's Drop Cloths, Blankets, and Curtains

If you're in a bind and want to cover something quickly because of incoming inclement weather, you can find 10 x 25-foot (3 x 7.5 m) sheets of clear 4-mil plastic in the paint department at your local hardware store. If frost warnings are broadcast, and your home center is out of rolls of 4- or 6-mil plastic, you can always find packages of plastic drop cloths, which won't last a long time, but will get plants through a tough time.

Professional painters use white canvas drop cloths, which can be purchased at professional paint supply outlets or in the paint section of hardware stores. An 8 x 10-foot (2.4 m x 3 m) canvas drop cloth is reasonably priced and light enough to fold into a fairly small bundle for storage. Coating one side of the canvas with a fabric guard (I use one of the types that can be sprayed from a pump can) gives excellent hard-weather protection and will allow the cloth to keep from absorbing moisture during prolonged freezing rains and snow.

If it's cold enough to put a second blanket on your own bed, it's cold enough to put another layer over your plants to give them protection until the cold spell has passed. You'll find that you can take plants through spells of really frigid weather if you cover them. Old blankets or curtains are great to use to cover plants inside your greenhouse. When used outside to cover warm-weather crops at the end of the summer (to see them through early frosts), you may need to add an additional waterproof covering, such as 6-mil plastic or a tarp.

One side of this double-sashed cold frame is covered with 6-mil, construction grade polyurethane with fencing stapled to the sash for structural integrity. The second sash is covered with floater and a blanket (to protect plants from approaching cold weather).

Floating Row Covers

See chapter 3 for more on this multifaceted covering.

Framing Material

You'll use one or more of the following materials to help you frame your tunnel, stoop house, or greenhouse.

PVC Pipe

PVC pipe is the common plumber's pipe that's found in home centers and lumberyards. It generally comes in 10-foot (3 m) lengths and various diameters. You may have to go to a plumbing-supply outlet to get full 20-foot (6 m) lengths. PVC comes in three thicknesses. "Schedule 40" is the thickness that's most appropriate for your gardening purposes and, as it turns out, it's usually the most readily available. "Schedule 80" PVC is much thicker than necessary

PVC pipe used to frame both a greenhouse and a tunnel

and costs more. There's another white pipe that's cheaper than "Schedule 40" pipe. It has one enlarged end to make continuous pieces by attaching pipes end-to-end without the use of junction connectors. This pipe is not good for season extension because it doesn't have the strength to hold up under snow loads.

There's some discussion about whether or not PVC breaks down over time under UV radiation. Plumbing supply outlets commonly store PVC outside where it's exposed to UV radiation, and plumbers I've spoken to have never experienced problems with pipes shattering. Be that as it may, you may wish to protect the PVC pipe with a good primer. There are several brands on the market that will stick to anything—even the slick surface of PVC.

A handsaw will cut through PVC very easily. One word of caution, however. If you're drilling holes through PVC, begin with a small pilot hole first, and increase the size of the hole progressively a couple of times to get to the dimension you need. This keeps stress cracks from starting.

PVC pipes will spring back into position if they've partially collapsed because of a heavy snow load. There's a potential to crush plants, but this can be easily fixed by brushing snow off with a broom.

Though I find it time consuming to bend EMT pipes so that they make uniform ribs, it can be accomplished by shaping each rib around a pre-made form. Photo by John Wilson

EMT Pipe

EMT pipe is the metal conduit that's used to cover electric wires when they're run outside walls in places where looks don't count. It can be found in a number of diameters in the electrical department of your local lumberyard or home center. It cuts easily with a hacksaw and cuts like a dream if you fit your circular saw with a metal-cutting blade (wear your safety goggles). Smaller dimensions of this pipe can be bent with a special pipe bender. There's also a dazzling array of connectors and junctions available for those interested in experimenting in making their own contraptions. There are certain uses for EMT in a greenhouse, but I don't use them for hoops.

Rebar

Concrete reinforcing bar (rebar) comes in several thicknesses and is used to reinforce patios and sidewalks made of poured concrete. It comes in 20-foot (60 m) lengths, and you can often have it cut cheaply at the lumberyard or home center where you bought it. It can also be purchased in shorter lengths. I use ½-inch (1.3 cm) rebar for stakes to hold up the sides of raised beds and also to create stoop houses. Rebar can be cut with a hacksaw, but it's much easier to cut with a metal-cutting blade on a circular saw. It isn't necessary to cut completely through the rebar—cut it halfway through and break it at the cut by bending it.

A Few Thoughts on Lumber

When choosing lumber for cold frames or other season extension contraptions, some people use pressure-treated wood so the frame won't rot as quickly as untreated lumber. I advise against this. Though treated for outside use, this lumber has been impregnated with, among other nasty chemicals, cyanide. Organic gardeners know the dangers of growing food near treated lumber. Readily available rot-resistant alternatives are cedar, cypress, and redwood. Locust is very rot-resistant, and some lumber mill operators will cut it for you (if locust trees grow in your region), although there's a mild toxin in locust sawdust that some sawmill operators are allergic to. I've used untreated and non-rot-resistant wood for many season extension projects. For cold frames, greenhouse framing, and the sides of raised beds, I've always used either the common untreated spruce framing lumber, unless I'm able to find a rot-resistant wood. Rough-cut, full dimension, 2-inch-thick (5.1 cm) pine, that's found at your local lumber mill, is very cost-effective and will last five to eight years before it needs to be replaced. For sash frames, doors, and vent frames, I've always used 1 x 3-inch (2.5 cm x 7.6 cm) spruce furring or simple 1 x 6-inch (2.5 x 15.2 cm) pine ripped to the width I need. Even in fairly humid environments, an untreated frame will last many years before the lumber rots.

When purchasing lumber, look carefully at a number of pieces in the pile you're picking from to get the best material; there's no reason to buy a piece of lumber that's hooked, cupped, or crowned. To check for straightness, pick up one end of a piece of lumber and look down one of the edges, then rotate the board to look at another edge; you'll see very clearly whether or not the board is straight. And don't buy lumber until you're ready to build your project; a piece of straight wood that sits around for a few weeks can quickly change shape because of moisture, temperature change, and improper stacking. If you're having lumber delivered to your home, look through the load when it's dropped off, and don't sign for it until you're satisfied with its condition. And send back pieces that aren't up to your standards of straightness.

Fencing

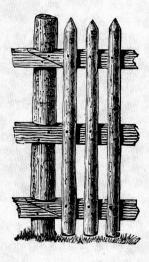

To give structural integrity to cold frame sashes, I sometimes use galvanized fencing that has 2 x 4-inch (5.1 x 10.2 cm) openings. I also use chicken wire for the same purpose, though I have found it more difficult to work with because it doesn't lie flat as easily. Both are easy to cut with wire cutters. Chicken wire works great when you want to cover vent openings to keep unwanted animals out of your greenhouse or cold frame.

Hardware

The contraptions that you'll assemble for use in your garden will be used during the harshest weather conditions of the year. It's for this reason that fastenings and hardware should be as durable as possible. While I'm willing to purchase the cheaper untreated lumber, I don't skimp when it comes to hardware. It's easy to be seduced into buying zinc- or brass-plated parts, especially when their labels read "weather resistant." They, however, will lose their protective covering, and fail when you need them to perform. Brass-plated hinges are fine for interior cabinets and doors; when installed outside, however, they're destined for a rusty demise (regardless of their "weather resistant" tags).

Instead, use galvanized hinges, screws, bolts, and miscellaneous hardware. You can find much pricier stainless steel or solid brass hardware that works just fine, but you'll find a wider array of styles of galvanized hardware from which to choose. I've used galvanized screen-door hinges with removable brass pins when I've had different sashes for the same cold frame. (Removing pins to change a solid plastic sash for a shade cloth-covered sash is very simple if you've purchased two pairs of the same type of hinge [with removable pins] and have installed them so both sashes fit the same permanently installed half-hinge parts on the cold frame.)

You can also find oddball pairs of hinges and parts that'll work for you in discount bins of hardware stores or in junk boxes out in grandpa's workshop. You'll even find solid brass hardware, but the challenge is telling the real thing from brass-plated impostors. Here's how you can tell the difference: Hold a refrigerator magnet to the brass hardware in question. If it's solid brass, it won't stick to the magnet; if it's an impostor, it'll stick.

HOOKS AND EYES

Doors on greenhouses and cold frame sashes need to be fastened tightly, or winter winds will open them up when you need them closed the most. But it's also handy to have hardware that'll securely hold doors and sashes ajar slightly to allow for a small amount of venting. Hook and eye fastenings with several different eye placements are a good solution for accomplishing double duty, especially if the hook is fitted with a simple, spring-loaded, sliding lock mechanism. You can take this a step further and install several different lengths of hooks that will allow you to keep your doors or sashes propped open narrowly, and at progressively wider spaces. I've used 2, 6, and 10-inch (5.1, 15.2 and 25.4 cm) hooks on one cold frame sash, and found it to be a pretty darn effective system. It's difficult to find 10-inch (25.4 cm) hooks, so buy several when you

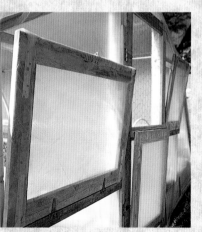

A pair of hooks and eyes holding a greenhouse vent open

do find them. Also, hook-and-eye systems should be used in pairs at the two outside points of the door or sash panel you're rigging to give equal support.

Framing Plates

Framing plates and straps are used during the framing phase of home construction to give additional integrity to the framing on homes. They're also intended to make various odd connections more secure with less effort. These plates come in many sizes, and they have a number of holes prepunched to allow you to connect them to your project however you need to. The #8 pan-head screw fits perfectly through the prepunched holes. These plates bend easily and cut readily with a metal-cutting blade in a jigsaw or circular saw, or with a simple hacksaw. You can use them to strengthen shaky window frames and to add structural integrity to wood-to-wood connections on your stoop house, tunnel, or greenhouse.

Bending Framing Plates

To bend a framing plate, hold or clamp the plate to the edge of a sturdy table. Don't clamp the plate until the location of the first bend is right at the edge. Hammer the part of the plate that's hanging off the table until you've created a right angle with a crisp edge. Then place the L-shaped plate on the table and fit the wood you're using inside the "L". You can attach the plate to the wood with a screw if you wish. Finally, hammer the plate until it's wrapped around the wood on three sides. Screw the plate to the piece of wood, and then attach the second piece of wood as needed.

Nails and Screws

Always use galvanized or stainless-steel nails and screws on your contraptions. Galvanized nails with rings or spirals on the shank will hold better than straight-shanked nails. Galvanized plasterboard screws come in many sizes and are easy to attach using a #2 Phillips-head bit on a variable speed drill. Framing plates can be attached using $^1/_2$-inch (1.3 cm), #8 stainless-steel, Phillips-head, pan-style screws. These screws are sometimes sold as sheet-metal screws that have a self-tapping tip (they don't require predrilling).

Glue

When glue is required to make a positive connection, purchase tubes of construction-grade glue that are applied using a glue gun. (An adequate glue gun can be purchased at a very low cost in the same aisle where you find the glue.) Also make sure you purchase glue that's rated for exterior purposes or subfloors. Remember that glue, regardless of how great it holds, is used only as double insurance on a wood-to-wood connection. Always use screws or nails in addition to the glue to achieve a totally bombproof connection that'll give you years of service.

Tool Chest

Most of the tools required for the projects in this book are probably already in your garage or basement.

SAFETY

Any time you're working with power tools, you should wear safety glasses. If you can see the moving blade of a saw (and you should see it if you want to make an accurate cut), your eyes will be in the field of flying wood or metal debris that's spraying out of the cut you're making. Safety glasses or goggles are not only a good idea for safety, but they're also a good idea if you want to ensure accuracy. I attach cords to my safety glasses (available wherever sunglasses are sold) so they hang around my neck, always within easy reach when I want to make a cut.

MEASUREMENT AND LAYOUT

A 25-foot (7.5 m) tape measure will work for all projects in this book, except for taking diagonals on the garden greenhouse. For this you should have a 100-foot (30 m) tape. If you don't want to purchase one, you may wish to call around to borrow one from carpenter friends. Or call an equipment rental outlet to see if one's available. You'll also need a carpenter's square or a framing square to mark lines for accurate cuts.

When Being Square Is Hip

Several times throughout this book you'll read that you must make something "square" by taking diagonal measurements. It's important for a greenhouse or a cold frame sash to be exactly square. When something is out-of-square it becomes a parallelogram. An example of "out-of-square" is a doorway in an old house where the floor has settled and is no longer level; the square door will no longer fit properly in the out-of-square doorway. If you put together a cold frame sash, and you don't make it square before tightening all the fastenings, it won't fit in the frame it's mounted to. And a greenhouse that doesn't begin with a square footprint will become a nightmare to assemble properly.

Taking diagonals

Fortunately, making something square is very easy. Measuring diagonally from one corner to the opposite corner on both sides does it. If the two measurements are the same, you can be assured the project is square. In figure 1 you'll see that the diagonal A-C is 100 inches (2.5 m) long. The diagonal B-D is 90 inches (2.3 m). To make the figure square, you need to move A-D toward the D corner until the diagonal is 95 inches (2.4 m).

Figure 1

Generally, when assembling a project that needs to be square, place a screw (or some other fastening) at each junction point to allow a certain degree of mobility, while still keeping it together. If the diagonal measurements are different when you take the two measurements, simply push to the longest corner back, half the distance of the difference between the two measurements, and then remeasure to make sure the diagonal measurements are the same.

CUTTING

You'll find that a handsaw and a hacksaw will be adequate for cutting wood and metal, but it'll be a strenuous and time-consuming job. A circular saw outfitted with a woodcutting blade (interchangeable with a metal-cutting blade) will make your projects much easier. A jigsaw with interchangeable blades is nice to have available, but not critical.

Drilling Holes and Driving Screws

You'll need a variable-speed $^3/_8$-inch drill to cut holes and drive screws. A cordless drill is really handy for installing pan-head screws because there's no cord to deal with, but it just doesn't have the power and speed to drill holes through metal or wood. If you're installing large nails, it's often easier to drill pilot holes first using a $^1/_8$-inch drill bit. When building the greenhouse, you'll also need to purchase a bit $^1/_{16}$-inch (1.6 mm) smaller than the bolts you plan to use. A $^5/_{16}$-inch (8 mm) bolt, for example, needs a $^1/_4$-inch bit to make the appropriate hole. You'll find that drilling holes through EMT pipe is easier if you begin with a $^1/_8$-inch (3 mm) hole and make two jumps up in size to the final size you want the hole to be. And make sure you purchase metal-cutting bits if you wish to cut through metal. A metal-cutting bit will cut through wood, but a woodcutting bit won't cut through metal. A #2 Phillips-head driver bit will drive galvanized plasterboard screws and the pan-head screws as well. Driving screws by hand with a screwdriver can be done, but it's tedious, at best, and is a quick way to sour a gardener's resolve to build season extenders.

Driving Stakes and Nails

You'll need a common carpenter's hammer for driving nails. It'll serve the purpose for driving rebar stakes as well, though some folks prefer a sledgehammer, which is definitely necessary for driving EMT pipe in the ground around the perimeter of your garden greenhouse.

Creating Level and Plumb Contraptions

Just because you may have never built a contraption before doesn't mean it has to look that way. A level is essential if you want a contraption that looks good and works well. You'll need one to install your cold frame and set up the vent openings of your garden greenhouse. Nothing makes a contraption look more amateurish than to have a cold frame out of level or doors on a greenhouse that aren't plumb (exactly perpendicular). If you have a 4-foot (1.2 m) level, your readings will be significantly more accurate than if you use a level that's shorter than 14 inches (35.6 cm). It's worthwhile to purchase a 3- or 4-foot (.9 to 1.2 m) level to get the end results you desire. Levels are delicate instruments and are notorious for losing their calibrations when dropped. If you borrow a level, make sure it reads accurately by trying it out on a known plumb surface like the side of a door in your house, and a known level surface like a countertop where an egg remains where it's set. Try it out in half a dozen different known level and plumb surfaces so you know that the bubbles in the level are reading accurately.

ATTACHING PLASTIC

A staple gun is an essential tool for attaching plastic to your stoop house, garden greenhouse, and cold frame sashes. It's also handy for attaching fencing temporarily over vents and sashes.

CUTTING WIRE

A heavy pair of wire cutters will make your life much simpler when you're cutting wire.

Strange Options for Sash Coverings

WHILE DRIVING DOWN THE HIGHWAY, you've probably seen house movers traveling with oversized loads of houses that have been cut in half. The open middle of these houses-in-transit is often covered with a heavy, white, plastic film. I have a friend who once found a bunch of this material at the landfill and brought it home to use for covering the firewood supply. He had a lot of the material and ended up using it in the fall and spring to cover plants during cold snaps as well. As it turns out, he also used it to cover a cold frame sash. In spite of the fact that you couldn't see through the plastic, it reflected a tremendous amount of light inside the frame. His white-plastic-covered cold frame produced as steady a supply of cold-hardy salad greens as any of his clear-sashed cold frames had ever done. From his observations, the white plastic kept the plants inside the frame from overheating because it reduced the amount of direct sunlight that came in, yet it allowed enough reflected light to bounce around the inside of the frame to produce salad greens.

FLOATERS AND ROW COVERS

IN MANY PARTS OF THE COUNTRY, early spring brings the promise of warm days. But it doesn't matter how warm the days are if the nights bring killer frosts. And in the mountains near Asheville, North Carolina where I live, frosts may linger past May 1, even though the days can get downright hot. Lettuce, spinach, and peas that are planted in early spring thrive during those warm days. It's under these circumstances that gardeners get lulled into a false sense of security. That's the time to be vigilant

It may not look pretty, but covering your garden rows and beds with floaters or row covers is an effective way to protect your plants. Fabric has simply been laid over the left row, while a row cover has been constructed for the row on the right.

The Many Ways to Use Floaters and Row Covers

§ They provide a first line of defense against frost. Floaters are wonderful for unexpected frosts because you simply lay them over your beds.

§ You can increase germination rates when you cover seedbeds with floaters or row covers.

§ Both provide an effective second layer of protection under other contraptions.

§ They can serve as protection for tender plants that don't like the heat. In addition, keeping your plants covered in the late winter and through the spring will moderate the temperatures during the warm days so your plants don't experience such wide temperature swings.

and make sure that each night finds your plants under protection. Whether you choose to simply cover your veggies with fabric or build any of the structures in this chapter, you'll find that these lightweight frost shields are easy to assemble and manage, and they're a perfect solution for combating a surprise frost.

Floaters (Floating Row Covers)

Floating row covers (referred to as "floaters" from here on out) are the perfect solution when you want to create an effective enhanced growing environment without spending a lot of money.

If you've ever had kittens in your house, I'm willing to bet that you've already seen the first generation of this season extension textile. Kittens love to crawl under couches and chairs and rip at the upholstery lining. The lining is usually dark colored and gauzelike. Back in the mid-1970s, tobacco farmers were looking for a protective covering for their early spring seedbeds to replace cotton sheets that had always been used before. Someone tried the white version of this upholstery backing, and it performed significantly better than the traditional cotton sheets. It was found that the thin, spun-bonded structure of the fabric dried out quickly after rain, and it boosted germination rates in an unexpected manner. It wasn't long before the fabric showed up in the home vegetable gardens of tobacco farmers.

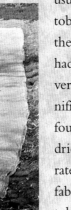

A seedbed of tobacco under a sheet of floater in late spring

Today, floaters can be found in garden centers, sometimes under the name "garden blanket." These white, gauzelike fabrics can be placed directly over the top of planted or seeded beds without damaging plants. They come in several thicknesses and have repeatedly been shown to increase germination rates, take the edge off wind damage, and supply several degrees of frost protection. Floaters will also produce a 1° to 2° advantage for warm-weather plants that are seeing the cusp of freezing temperatures in early fall. But for cold-hardy plants surviving in hard-freeze conditions, floaters produce a surprisingly effective environment, allowing plants to remain undamaged until warmer temperatures return.

Floaters are simply laid over sown beds and transplants. Air, sunlight, and water will penetrate through the surface of floaters, and as plants grow, they push the loose fabric up. You'll find it remarkable at first that plants are undamaged by this contact. As long as the edges of the fabric are held down, you'll get excellent protection for your plants. And besides being *de rigueur* for season

Boards and rocks are used to trap pieces of floater over raised beds.

extension, lighter-weight models are also an effective barrier against cabbage loopers, Colorado potato beetles, and other invasive pests, when kept in place for the entire growing season. When the fabric is hung loosely with the bottom edges sealed, summer plants will push against it as they grow undamaged, and critters will simply be unable to do their damaging work.

How long you leave floaters in place is a matter of personal preference. You can leave light-gauge floaters in place all summer, because they'll moderate hot temperatures as well. But unless I'm using them for pest control in warm weather, I put them away when the threat of frost is gone, because I want to extend the life expectancy of the fabric.

FLOATER SIZE CONSIDERATION

Floaters come in a variety of sizes. Some gardeners use 25-foot-wide (7.5 m) pieces (or larger) and cover whole sections of the garden without using ribs (see Row Covers on page 35). This puts everything under cover, including pathways, and creates a slightly warmer microenvironment. This works great in the spring if you've just seeded or transplanted into a large area and won't be working the ground there for two to four weeks (until the plants have really taken hold). And seedlings won't generally suffer the same freeze burn that you'll notice on mature plants when ice-soaked floaters touch leaves. It's easy to hold edges down with boards that have rocks or some other weights on them. Once your plants have taken hold, though, this method of coverage is impractical if you have a number of different crops growing, because as they mature, they'll require different growing environments and maintenance.

Floaters also come in 5-foot (1.5 m) widths, which is fine if you're only buying them to cover seedbeds. The 10-foot (3 m) width allows for more possibilities. But the reality of a busy, hardy gardener dictates that there will be times when you don't have the luxury of a roll of floater in the garden shed, and you'll be darn happy to find any size you can at the local garden supply. Quite often, prepackaged floater material at the local garden center will come in 20 x 25-foot (6 x 7.5 m) blankets. When I get it this size, I immediately cut it to the sizes I need and roll them into individual bundles. With bundles ready, I don't need to fumble around with a piece that's twice as wide as I need. Also, the 5-foot-wide (1.5 m) pieces can be sewn together if that's the only width you can find.

TAKING CARE OF YOUR FLOATERS

If you take care of your floaters, you can get several seasons' use from them. You can extend the useful life of your fabric by watching for areas that have been torn by wind and rough handling. Placing scrap sections of old fabric over exposed areas in the torn floaters will extend the life expectancy considerably. I've even sewn small pieces of old floater over rips, using a needle and waxed dental floss. If you patch or stitch every tear, your efforts will give you a solid three years of hard use, provided you start with the heaviest weight of floater. But the reality of hardy gardening is that your floater will tear when it's cold because you're trying to hurry, and the last thing you want to do is to fumble with a needle and a thread. In these situations, I grab pieces of old floater that I keep in a box and lay them over the torn area. Patch pieces should be large enough to secure with the same bricks, pegs, or clothespins that hold the rest of the fabric in place. I throw away pieces smaller than 4 x 4 feet (1.2 x 1.2 m). If you're gardening frugally, your floaters will look a bit ragged by the end of the second season, but your vigilance will be paid off by a better quality of veggie.

When I'm done with my floaters for the season, I fold them up and put them in a box on the shelf in the basement. After a couple years of using and cutting up floaters and salvaging pieces, you'll have a collection of various sizes. It's worthwhile to mark the size of each piece on the edge of the folded bundle with a heavy black marker when you put them away. I also mark the weight of the piece ("heavy" or "light") when it goes into storage. When you open up the box to grab a sheet of floater, you'll appreciate knowing the size and weight of the piece you're grabbing.

It's important that you understand the fundamentals of using floaters, because they're the versatile workhorses of your hardy garden. Throughout the rest of this book, you'll find that you can make use of floaters in conjunction with various strategies and contraptions to increase their effectiveness.

Row Covers

Although "floating row cover" is the term used to identify the fabric that I've just talked about in the previous section, you'll also hear just the words "row cover" when folks talk about season extension. The term is different from a floating row cover, but not unrelated. Confused? Here's the difference: A "floating row cover" is the fabric, and a "row cover" is a device that arches over a row or bed in the garden and is generally covered with floating row cover, which is why I refer to floating row covers as "floaters."

So, if a floater is light enough to simply lay over plants in the garden, why would you need to use it in conjunction with the structure of a row cover to arch it over the top of the garden? Once you begin using floaters, you'll notice that wherever plants touch the fabric after a freezing rain, there will often be freeze burns on the plant's surface. The remedy for this is to set up a wire frame over the growing area. Cover the frame with a floater, and you've got a row cover.

ROW COVER RIBS

There are many different materials you can use to create ribs, and which one you decide to use depends on the size of your garden and the availability of the material.

Double use of 9-gauge wire ribs with floater and a second layer of plastic insulation thrown on top

Nine-Gauge Wire

Where I live, you can buy rolls of this wire at local feed stores because so many local farmers use it for season extension in the fall and spring. To span a 40-inch (1 m) garden bed, cut the wire into 9-foot (2.7 m) lengths. Set these ribs 3 or 4 feet (.9 or 1.2 m) apart, and put two of these wire ribs at each location. The beauty of this system is that the floater material is sandwiched between each pair of wires to keep the fabric in place. If the top wire crosses slightly diagonally over the lower wire, you can slide the edge of the floater up when harvesting and it will hold in position. This same friction fit at each pair of ribs also keeps the fabric closed very effectively.

Block Ladders

These are 8- to 10-feet-long (2.4 to 3 m) wire ladders. The ladderlike configuration of these ribs gives them excellent strength when spanning a garden bed. They're made of wire $1/8$ inch (3 mm) in diameter and are traditionally used to embed into the cement between courses of cement cinder blocks to give walls structural integrity. They can usually be found in the masonry section of your lumberyard or home center. If you can't find them there, try a brick and cinder block outlet. Block ladders come in various widths, any of which will work. They look very much like wire ladders found in the season extension section of some garden supply catalogs, but block ladders are considerably larger and significantly less expensive. They'll span a 4-foot-wide (1.2 m) bed very easily, and they can be cut with heavy wire cutters to shorten them to span narrower beds. I often wire cut-off ends together to create ribs. I've found that the cut ends usually catch on floaters and rip the fabric unless I soften the points by covering them with bits of duct tape.

A bed of salad greens are being thinned in an early spring garden. Note how the block ladder ribs are bent to maximize the coverage of the bed.

The best aspect of using block ladders is the fact that you can bend them to have vertical sides rather than curved sides like hoops. Vertical sides allow for fuller use of a garden bed because plants at the edge of the growing space aren't crowded by the angle of the sides of the ribs when they're in hoop configuration. However, with the block ladders, you don't have the secure friction fit that results in the double use of 9-gauge wire ribs. So when you cover these block ladders with floater, you need to keep the fabric attached with clothespins spread out evenly on each rib. You also need bricks or boards to keep the bottom edges on the ground.

Concrete Reinforcing Wire

Another product that can be found in the masonry supply section of home centers is concrete reinforcing wire. This fencelike material comes in rolls 5 feet (1.5 m) wide with square openings sized 6 x 6 inches (15.2 x 15.2 cm). Many gardeners cut sections of this wire 12 squares long (making pieces of the fencing that have 10 openings along one side and 12 openings along the other side) to make tomato cages. In the spring, tomato cages can be covered with plastic film or floater to create an enhanced growing environment for newly planted tomatoes. As the tomato plants grow, the covering is removed so the cage can support the vines. In the fall, these cages can be loosened and spread out to make a cover that spans a 3-foot (.9 m) bed very nicely. This is a great frame to cover with floater material, and clothespins will again keep the fabric in place. The bottom edges of the fencelike frame can be held to the ground by slipping stones through the bottom rungs of the fencing or by staking the bottom edge to the ground with wooden stakes along the edge.

Low-Budget Alternatives to Floaters

Ever on the lookout for cost-effective alternatives to gardening equipment, I have tried various floater substitutions. One such alternative I've tested is septic line paper. You'll find rolls of this thin, gauzelike material (sometimes called "sewer wrap") in the plumbing department of your local home center or lumberyard. This fabric is used to wrap septic lines during installation to keep silt from collecting in the pipes. It comes in black and white; you want to get the white material. This fabric comes in 2-, 3-, and 4-foot (.6, .9, and 1.2 m) widths, and appears to be made of the same spun-bonded material as floaters. I've found that it works well, though it's considerably thinner than the more expensive

garden blanket. The 4-foot (1.2 m) maximum width is also a drawback. Though septic line paper can be purchased by the lineal foot, I bought a full roll one year because it was so inexpensive. I found the width a frustration when covering hoops over beds because it wasn't wide enough to span a bed over wire ribs without having a seam at the top, where it was vulnerable to winds. (Using the double rib system of 9-gauge wire is helpful in keeping this alternative fabric in place.) In addition, the fabric is fragile and tears easily in winds that hit my hillside garden site. The tear factor is reduced somewhat by placing double and triple thicknesses over the beds. This fabric definitely created an adequate enhanced growing environment, but I went back to using traditional floaters when my roll was used up (though I'll buy the sewer wrap if I'm in a bind and there are no other alternatives).

Yanna Fishman, a gardener I know, has found another alternative to floaters that extend the season in the same manner. Yanna goes to thrift stores and finds old curtains that have thin, veil-like cotton liners. These liners are removed from the curtains and used like floaters. They're the perfect width to span a bed and of a length that's easy to handle. They give the same protection as floaters and have a significantly longer life expectancy in the garden. The curtains are saved to give plants a second cover of protection on especially cold nights.

Final Thoughts on Floaters and Row Covers

In my garden, I have different crops growing in separate beds, and I choose to cover them independently in each bed from the beginning. It's worthwhile for me to order a 10 x 50-foot (3 x 15 m) roll of floater because that width will swathe my 3- to 4-foot-wide (.9 to 1.2 m) beds, with or without the support of ribs. The extra fabric on each side of the bed provides a surface where I can place stones or bricks to secure the floater to the ground. That extra fabric on each side also allows for sloppy placement of the fabric, which is an issue when you're trying to cover up 500 square feet (45 m²) of bed, ribs, and plants when there's a stiff wind blowing (a common situation encountered in winter gardening). You can get by with only 2 or 3 extra inches (5.1 or 7.6 cm) on each side for placing the hold-down weight, but it requires careful alignment when you're covering a long run of ribs to make sure the whole rig's buttoned up. The extra material on each side will give you a margin of error, which allows you to get your plants covered up in challenging conditions without its being a frustration. There are pins available to keep the edges in place, but I've found that putting holes in the edges of floaters will cause rips to begin and eventually shorten the fabric's life.

❦ When using row covers, you'll find there are challenges in buttoning up the ends. The best way is to have enough floater to cover up the ends and then hold both sides down with a few rocks or bricks.

❦ You can make your row covers as long as you wish. There are modern market gardeners who cover whole fields with these contraptions in the late winter and early spring. Plastic films are also a practical substitution if floater material is unavailable when you need it.

Common sense is your greatest ally in season extension. If the forecast calls for frigid weather, you can take steps to improve the protection that's already in place. Hardy though they are, winter veggies will love an extra layer of protection and will recover more quickly to grade A condition when more moderate winter temperatures return. You can improve the floater's protecting ability by adding another layer of material, such as curtains, tarps, and 4- to 6-mil plastic over the wire ribs on really frigid nights. A commonsense approach to season extension dictates that you should always be thinking of ways to improve the performance of other contraptions that you'll be learning about later in this book, and floaters are your best investment for making other contraptions better.

A piece of floater used over a raised bed to protect cold-hardy crops in an unfinished greenhouse

Tunnels and Stoop Houses

THOUGH I LIKE TO THINK IT'S NOT THE CASE, my actions have consistently shown that I've always striven to make enterprises in the garden as complicated as possible. This is certainly the case with season extension contraptions; there's such a wonderful variety of pipes, fabrics, and totally swell gizmos (all manufactured for other purposes) that begs folks who have overly active imaginations to use them in the garden. And I'm not the only one who's been seduced into elaborate season extension schemes. Over the years, I've had countless conversations with folks who have gone through the same learning curve of season extension contraption incarnations (usually fueled by prowling the aisles and back lots of lumberyards searching for ways to use materials intended for other purposes). It took me about eight years to come up with the most effective way to enhance the growing environment of the most amount of planted real estate for the least outlay of cash. And two of the most effective ways I've found to extend the gardening season include using tunnels and stoop houses.

Tunnels

Some folks refer to tunnels and row covers interchangeably, but I'm going to make a distinction between the often lighter-gauge row cover structures and the slightly heavier tunnel structures. Tunnels are truly miniature, mobile greenhouses that easily span a 4-foot-wide (1.2 m) bed. They're made by bending a series of 10-foot-long (3 m) ribs over the top of a garden bed and covering the resulting frame with plastic. Modern-day, small-scale market gardeners use them

because the components are affordable, simple to assemble, easily expandable, and effective in creating enhanced growing environments. Tunnels also stand tall enough to protect big, robust kale and mustard. In fact, floaters and row covers can be used in conjunction with tunnels as additional "blankets" in colder climates.

The Many Ways to Use a Tunnel

§ You can protect hardy veggies that were planted in late summer from approaching cold weather.

§ In Zones 3 and 4 you can overwinter hardy veggies that were planted in late fall. When spring arrives, the already emerged (or ready-to-emerge) seedlings are protected.

§ You can protect plants placed in the garden before the threat of frost has passed in early spring.

§ In colder zones, you can enhance the growing environment around tender plants that suffer from the cooler nights of summer in Zones 3 and 4. In this case, they're also often used with a black plastic or stone mulch to raise soil temperatures.

TUNNEL DESIGNS

From a distance, all tunnels look the same and are generally covered with the same 6-mil plastic. The difference in tunnels is in the material used for the ribs that hold up the covering. I've used most of the variations described here, and there are good reasons for using each. The type of ribs you choose to use will probably be based on what you're able to find.

PVC Pipe Ribs

My first row cover ribs were made of 10-foot (3 m) lengths of ³/₄-inch (1.9 cm) PVC pipes that came from the plumbing department at the local hardware store. Ten feet (3 m) is the most commonly available length, and as it turns out, that's the perfect size to span a 4-foot-wide (1.2 m) area. I easily spanned and arched the PVC over my 4-foot (1.2 m) raised beds. I attached them to the wooden side-boards of the beds with galvanized plumbing

This photo shows the bracket used to attach the PVC rib to the wooden side of the raised bed, as well as the clamps used to attach the plastic to the rib.

brackets. Folks who don't have wooden sides on their beds can still use ³/₄-inch (1.9 cm) PVC ribs by sliding the ends over ¹/₂-inch (1.3 cm) rebar stakes. Simply drive the stakes into the ground at an angle on each side of the bed.

I use clear 6-mil construction-grade plastic, 12-feet (3.6 m) wide, to go over the arching PVC. I hold the edges down with rocks and cut slits in the top, which allows the tunnel to vent with the ends closed. Cutting slits in the top of a long tunnel facilitates hot air release and won't present a problem with wind as long as the bottom edges of the tunnel are secured to the ground. In fact, there are tunnel plastics sold commercially that have slits already in them to be used to cover long tunnels.

A lighter gauge rib can be made out of 10-foot (3 m) lengths of ¹/₂-inch (1.3 cm) PVC pipe. If you're using rebar stakes to make the pipe-to-ground connection, you'll find that ³/₈-inch (1 cm) rebar fits perfectly inside these pipes.

There are clips available that are made to slip over PVC pipe (specifically for holding plastic on tunnel structures), and these work well.

Using PVC Fittings with PVC Pipe

Some folks like using PVC pipe for tunnels because they can use fittings to make special frames for protecting plants. Barney Webster, of Wickford, Rhode Island, covers his pond in the fall with PVC hoops that are assembled using PVC plumbing connections where four pipes meet at one point. Before it's time to put a plastic cover over the hoop-covered pond to protect semitender

water plants through the winter, Barney uses the frame to support a netting that keeps fall leaves from getting into the pond and changing the pH of the water. Using fittings like this is a great idea because it allows you to span areas up to 8 feet (2.4 m) wide with a device that'll hold together in frigid weather. You should be advised that contraptions assembled in this manner don't have the structural integrity to keep from buckling from repeated snow loads. If you're in an area that receives heavy snowfall, you shouldn't make PVC season extenders held together with plumbing fittings.

In fact, even PVC pipe ribs used without fittings will sag under a heavy snow load, although they'll generally spring back into place when the load's gone. In areas where snowstorms are common, most hardy gardeners will brave the elements to brush accumulating snow from a tunnel with a broom. However, if you live in an area that gets heavy snow, you should use rebar for rib construction.

Concrete Re-enforcing Bar (Rebar)

Rebar hoops will last for decades. Their ends can be easily stuck into the ground, they're very cost-effective, and they never become fragile from UV radiation (as PVC may do). Ten-foot (3 m) rebar hoops placed 3 or 4 feet (.9 or 1.2 m) apart are a great way to cover 4-foot-wide (1.2 m) beds. Once one end of a 10-foot-long (3 m) rebar section is placed into the ground, the rebar bends easily to form a hoop. Twelve-foot-wide (3.6 m) 6-mil plastic fits perfectly over such frames and allows enough room to keep the bottoms of the plastic in place with rocks. One problem with rebar is that it's quite a bit heavier than PVC and will scratch the heck out of your car if you tie pieces to the roof to carry them home from the lumberyard. If you don't have racks on your vehicle, have the lumberyard deliver the rebar to your home; the modest delivery fee will be cheaper than a new paint job.

There's really no clip that will keep plastic attached to rebar, but rebar has a rough surface that'll hold plastic coverings if the edges are held down with rocks or bricks.

Another benefit of using rebar for tunnels is that they can be straightened out easily after using them. They make sturdy pole bean tepees in the summer.

EMT Pipe

Walk through the electrical department of a hardware store, and you'll find aluminum conduit called EMT pipe, which is used to sheath electrical wires. It looks like a great material to retrofit for tunnels because the aluminum is light enough to handle, and it won't rust in hard weather. You can bend conduit with a special bending tool, or by making a jig for that purpose, and some folks have made some excellent greenhouse frames using EMT conduit. I continue to harbor fantasies of making a cloche using EMT and these terrific little EMT joint connectors that are available. But for tunnel frames, my investigations have found tunnel ribs made of aluminum conduit produce nonuniform ribs when

someone other than an electrician tries bending the conduit into hoops of the size to span garden beds. So unless you're an electrician (or know one), you'll probably waste a lot of time trying to create EMT ribs that work for you.

DESIGNING THE ENDS TO CLOSE

When you set up a tunnel, you'll discover that you must do something to cover the ends of the tunnel. It's the same problem discussed with the row covers, but it's a bigger issue here because the tunnels stand taller than row covers and create a lot more plastic to deal with. You can fold the ends over and hold them

down with rocks and bricks, but that doesn't contribute to structural integrity. One really excellent method is to leave an extra 4 feet (1.2 m) of material at each end, gather the material at each end into balls, and wrap and tie the gathered balls with strong cord. Then, pull the cords tight in opposite directions from both ends and attach to stakes set 3 feet (1.5 m) from the tunnel. This system puts the plastic in tension, pulls it tight against the ribs, and improves the structural integrity of the whole tunnel.

VENTING AND WATERING

A plastic-covered tunnel won't allow water inside even if you've put slits in the plastic covering for venting. You should set up drip hoses to water the plants in your tunnel, especially when used during the summer months in Zone 3 or 4 to grow tender plants.

Stoop Houses

The system I've found to be wonderfully effective and easy to assemble spans three of my garden beds at one time. I use 20-foot (6 m) pieces of rebar, and I place the arching pieces 4 feet (1.2 m) apart as they span the beds. A frame made this large is actually an honest-to-goodness, low-budget greenhouse that can be assembled in an afternoon. Remaining true to my cheapskate nature, this season extension affair flies low to the ground in cost and technology, in a realm where expenses can skyrocket quickly with high-tech materials. I've used this system on and off over the years, and the beauty of it lies in the fact that it covers the most amount of real estate for the least amount of money. As I said, it covers three of my gar-

den beds at once, plus, it's big enough for me to walk about. I use the phrase "walk about" loosely because the structure's about 5 feet (1.5 m) tall in the center, forcing most folks to stoop when entering the structure. It's for this reason that I refer to this excellent season extension contraption as a stoop house.

The beauty of a stoop house lies not only in the fact that you can work inside this enhanced growing environment, but that you can also use floaters or row covers to span beds inside the structure. Plus, in the spring, your stoop house can be disassembled quickly. I store my rebar on a path next to my asparagus where I don't often walk for most of the year; it's out of the way, and

THE MANY WAYS TO USE A STOOP HOUSE

5 You can create a large enhanced environment over a large area.

5 You can plant cold-hardy plants in the late fall, and they'll flourish throughout the winter.

5 When summer approaches in Zones 3 and 4, you can use the stoop house with an open vented top to grow cucumbers, tomatoes or other warm-weather crops.

5 During the summer, you can dismantle the stoop house or use it for planting fall crops earlier than usual.

the rusty metal's hardly noticed. And the stoop house's total area of bed coverage is significantly more per dollar spent than other row cover systems I've used that span only one bed.

BUILDING YOUR STOOP HOUSE

To create a 16-foot-long (4.8 m) stoop house that covers three 15-foot-long (4.5 m) beds, you'll need the following materials and tools.

Materials and Tools

- 6 pieces of $^1/_2$-inch (1.3 cm) or $^3/_8$-inch (1 cm) rebar, 20 feet (6 m) long
- 26 strips of 1 x 2 pine lath, 8 feet (2.4 m) long
- Roll of wire (found with rebar in lumberyards, for wiring rebar together)
- Sheet of 6-mil construction-grade plastic, 10 x 65 feet (3 x 19.7 m)
- Variable-speed drill
- Wire cutters
- Pliers
- Staple gun with staples

Setting Up the Ribs

🍃 Stick one end of a piece of rebar into the ground about 6 inches (15.2 cm) deep on one side of the area to be covered. Bend the piece over and punch it into the ground on the far side of the area to be covered. Once you place one end of the rebar into the ground, it'll stay there if you maintain a steady hold on the metal rod and don't move it around too much.

🍃 Set up the rest of the rebar hoops over the beds, slightly less than 4 feet (1.2 m) apart.

Strengthening the Frame

🍃 Starting at the bottom of one of the sides where the ground meets the hoops, measure 10 to 15 inches (25.4 to 38.1 cm) above the ground, and run one of the pine lath pieces perpendicular to the hoops so that it touches the first three hoops (see figure 1). Where each hoop touches wood, drill a $^1/_4$-inch (6 mm) hole through the wood. Run a piece of wire through each of the holes and around the rebar and wood, and tighten the wire with the pliers.

🍃 Attach a second lath to the last three hoops (starting from the other end). This will leave a space in the middle. Place a third lath in the middle that overlaps the first two laths.

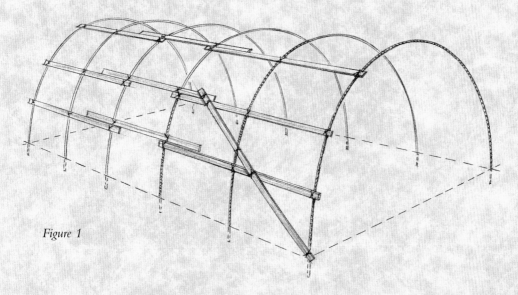

Figure 1

§ Repeat this process 30 inches (77 cm) above the row of laths you just attached. Repeat with a third set of laths 30 inches (77 cm) above the second row.

§ Repeat this procedure on the other side. Very quickly you'll notice excellent structural integrity as the tunnel becomes tied together in a web of hoops and laths.

§ When you've gone up three rows on each side, install one piece of lath at each corner of the frame, and run them at 45° angles (creating an upside-down "v" on both sides [see figure 1]). Wire the four laths at each intersection of wood and/or rebar to give the structure added strength. At this point you should have a very sweet, oversized frame covering your beds.

This stoop house frame is fully braced and ready to be covered.

Framing the Ends

§ You now need to install vertical pieces of lath to both ends of the tunnel. Begin on one end and mark off the center (highest point) of the hoop. Measure 15 inches (38.1 cm) on both sides of the center mark and mark the two locations. This is where the two vertical laths will be placed (see figure 2).

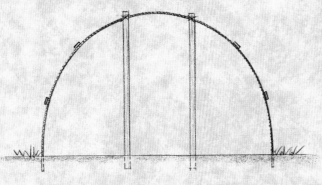

§ Push the bottom ends of the two wood laths into the ground, and attach the top ends to the rebar hoop where they intersect (use the same hole and wire system that you used for the sides). Cut the excess off the vertical pieces where they stick out above the hoops. These vertical pieces will be 30 inches (77 cm) apart. Repeat on the other end.

Figure 2

Covering the Stoop House

§ You could cover the whole frame with plastic, and I've done this in the past. But the busy schedules of folks today often make it necessary to leave the top of the house uncovered to allow hot air to escape while you're gone during the heat of midday. This means that your stoop house will have plastic going up the sides about 6 feet (1.8 m).

Floaters covering winter crops inside a stoop house

§ Use the staple gun to attach the 6-mil plastic to the wood laths. Because you're using 6-mil plastic that comes in 10-foot-wide (3 m) rolls, you can double the bottom 4 feet (1.2 m) to give added protection at plant level. The top edge of the plastic should land on the third band of horizontal lath from the bottom where you can staple off the plastic edge.

§ In colder zones, you may wish to make the opening in the top narrower to let air out. To do this, run two more strips of lath at the top, 6 inches (15.2 cm) apart. Attach them and secure the plastic to these laths instead. You can also cover this structure entirely, but you'll find that you need to set up some sort of venting system out the ends. From my experience, it's just as easy to vent out the top. You won't suffer damage from wind if you staple the plastic securely onto the lath where the vent slot begins.

§ The vertical laths are already in place on the ends and are ready to be covered with plastic. Make certain that you leave an opening on the southern end to allow entry. It doesn't need to have a door, as long as you can slide through an opening left between two of the vertical pieces.

§ Create a flap door by attaching a piece of plastic that overlaps the sides to the top of the door frame. Leave extra plastic at the bottom so you can place rocks on top of the plastic door to keep it in place.

All of the wooden and metal parts of this structure can be used for many years, so it's a good investment. As an unfortunate compromise, the plastic will need to be replaced each year.

Stoop House Considerations

§ The beauty of this open-topped affair is that it allows rain and snow to enter, so the plants don't need extra water. However, keep an eye on the plants closest to the edges of the hoops, which are often protected from this natural watering.

§ The opening in the top of this structure should make you more conscious of the needs of your winter greens to be covered as colder weather approaches. Install row covers over the beds inside the stoop house to give them extra cover. You can also put a tunnel over the row covers to add another layer of protection.

§ Your stoop house can cover two wide raised beds, three narrower raised beds, or a space in the garden that measures 13 or 14 feet (3.9 or 4.2 m) wide (and however long you wish to make it). It's critical that you determine which part of the garden you want this contraption to cover by midsummer, so you can begin planting fall crops in late summer as your summer crops (in warmer zones) or spring crops (in colder zones) are being harvested.

§ As you plan the beds that'll be under the cover of your stoop house, consider planting one bed that will produce food the latest, and cover it with the most layers of protection. As the winter progresses, eat first from the beds with less protection.

Notice the extra bracing used on the closed-up end wall.

Cloche Encounters

A CLOCHE IS LIKE A TINY GREENHOUSE that sits on a garden bed. They're perfect for growing transplant stock from seed, as detailed later in this chapter, and starting warm-weather plants early. The first bell-shaped glass cloches were invented in 1623 in Italy and were generally about 17 inches (43.2 cm) in diameter and 15 inches (38.1 cm) tall. Modern cloches are simple to make and even simpler to use, and understanding their potential should be in every high-performance gardener's bag of tricks for extending the season.

The original cloche design and function have changed very little over the last 350 years. Variations that have come into fashion over time include carrying knobs on top, venting holes, and tinted colors to reduce heat. But the basic

shape has remained the same. Today there's a wide range of cloche designs: homemade newspaper hats, 3-foot-tall (.9 m) plastic cones, commercially available waxed paper caps, panes of glass that form a diminutive barnlike structure, water-filled conical tubes, and many more.

Cloches don't take up a lot of space because they can usually be stacked easily for storage, and they accomplish work for you that just can't be done as effectively in a cold frame or a greenhouse. In addition, cloches can be used inside tunnels, cold frames, and greenhouses in more extreme climates to add a second layer of protection.

If you want to spend the cash, you can easily be seduced into buying some very cool looking cloches that are on the market today, but they won't work

any better than more humble cloches that you can get for a song. One gardener in Zone-5 Wakefield, Rhode Island, plants half his tomatoes and peppers under homemade cloches on April 1, and he uses several cloche designs: gallon-sized (3.8 L) plastic wine jugs (with the bottoms removed) that came from the local bowling alley, 3-gallon (11.4 L) food-grade buckets that came from the local bakery, bottomless milk or bleach jugs, and 5-gallon (19 L) plasterboard joint compound buckets that came from a carpenter friend. The white buckets have a 1-inch (2.5 cm) hole drilled in the top to allow venting. For several weeks, his warm-weather tomatoes and peppers can grow inside the buckets and jugs because their needs are being met by reflected light inside the white interiors rather than direct sunlight. Skeptical about the effectiveness of his cloche system in protecting warm-weather plants from frost, I visited his garden the morning after outside temperatures had dropped to 26°F (-3°C). Except where the leaves of plants touched the inside of the cloches, I found to my amazement that the plants suffered no problems. On several occasions, when the temperatures dropped mightily, this fellow lost all the plants that he set out under his cloches. That's why he plants only half of the tomato and pepper seedlings he starts under lights under cloches. But when the gamble pays off, he's able to get three weeks of extra harvest on those heat-loving plants.

Water-filled conical cloches
Photo by Sue Waterman

Cloche Basics

As I've said before, cloches are simple to use and quite effective in extending the garden season; however, there are some factors to consider when using them.

VENTING

Sunshine will cause air to heat up inside cloches, so all designs require some sort of venting capacity. For hundreds of years, market gardeners kept their thousands of cloches from overheating with a wooden gizmo called a "cloche tilt." The French *maraichers* called them *"fourchettes."* At the very least, these folks had to raise each cloche on these tilts in the morning before the sunlight became intense and lower them at night before the cold crept in. During the day, they also had to keep track of changing temperatures and respond accordingly. On windy days, they had to make sure tilted cloches didn't drop into a closed position and suffocate the plants inside. And all this monitoring had to be done while they were taking care of all the other responsibilities of growing, harvesting, and marketing the fruit and veggies produced in an intensively planted small garden.

Alas, most of us are unable to spend each of our days working in our gardens, but our cloches still need to have the ability to vent when necessary. My plants have suffered more damage due to overheating in season extension contraptions than they have when it got a bit too chilly. It's because of this that I like to err on the cold side in case I miscalculate on changing weather conditions before I head off to work in the morning.

The Many Ways to Use a Cloche

I don't have 3,000 glass cloches (the number of glass, bell-shaped cloches typically owned by late 19th-century market gardeners), or even the 100 recommended by more than one gardening manual I've read from the early 20th century. I don't even *want* that many cloches, and my busy schedule dictates that I wouldn't be around to babysit the cloches to keep them from overheating. But even if you only use a few cloches, you'll still benefit from their superior protection:

꽃 Regardless of the type that you use, cloches are very effective for covering individual tender plants that are set out in the garden before the threat of frost has passed.

꽃 You can give warm-weather plants a head start. Tomatoes, as well as newly planted squash, melon, and peppers, benefit greatly from the enhanced growing environment of cloches in the first couple weeks in your garden. These warm-weather plants especially benefit from the warmer soil temperatures inside the cloches, which accelerate germination rates. If you combine a cloche with stone mulch (see page 116) you can improve the microclimate around your plants even more significantly.

꽃 Also, the same tomatoes that benefit from the warm environment of a cloche after the threat of frost has passed, will survive seven out of ten seasons if you plant them at least a couple of weeks before the last frost. When the gamble pays off, you'll reap the rewards of earlier fruiting and a longer harvest. And if you lose plants because of unseasonably late hard freezes, you can still plant again when your less adventurous neighbors are planting.

꽃 You can create your own propagation plot (see The Tiny Plot Propagation System on page 58).

Various modern commercial cloche designs allow for hot air to escape by keeping a hole in the top. Cutting 2-inch (5.1 cm) holes in the top of white 5-gallon (11.4 L) bucket cloches and taking the caps off wine bottle cloches will allow for adequate venting in colder zones. Cutting a couple more holes in the tops of buckets or plastic jugs is necessary in Zone 6, where it's warm enough for cloche interiors to heat up more. You can tell your plants need more venting if they wilt. I've seen photos in some gardening manuals that show 1-quart (.95 L) jars placed upside down over immature plants to provide a form of cloche protection. I question whether the authors of these books have actually used these small jars for this purpose, because their interiors are so small that they're guaranteed to overheat quickly, and there's no venting capacity.

WATERING

Another challenge when working with cloches is the need to water more often than in other, larger season extension contraptions. It should be noted that "watering more often" is a relative term in the winter garden. In general, I water my winter plants one-tenth as much as I water my summer garden. But in relationship to plants in other types of contraptions, you'll need to water more often. Old-time gardeners using glass cloches poured water over the cloches and let capillary action draw water to the plants inside. Rain or snow also got to the plants through capillary action. Keep an eye on your protected plants and know that higher temperatures inside cloches will cause the soil to dry faster. Also remember to water in the morning so your plants aren't spending the cold night in overly moist conditions.

BATTLING THE WIND

A third challenge to be aware of when using cloches is that they can fly away on windy days. Some designs allow you to use a rock to hold down the base. Sometimes I create long staples from tiger teeth (24-inch [61 cm] pieces of rigid wire used to hold wall insulation in place) or use some other form of heavy wire to penetrate the cloches to keep them from blowing away. Sometimes cloches can remain earthbound by mounding soil around the base. Whatever methods you come up with, it's important that you do it, because one lapse in vigilance on a cold, windy night can cause weeks of nurturing plants under cover to go to waste.

Cloche Designs

The first cloche I used for starting transplant stock was a commercially produced contraption made from clear rigid plastic fastened into a cone with an open top to let hot air out and moisture in. These cones were made to perform in Zone 4, but they worked perfectly throughout the winter in Zone 5 southern New England. However, when I moved to the mountains of North Carolina, where it's generally Zone 6, I found that the cones got too hot, and they baked my seedlings several times. Typical winters in the mountains where I live can see temperatures drop down far below freezing at night and rise up to 60°F (16°C) during the day. This wide temperature fluctuation forced me to rig a cloche design that allowed for both extremes, while still producing quality transplant stock.

LAMPSHADE CLOCHE

Old or discarded lampshades are easy to find at places like yard sales, flea markets, thrift stores, or even along streets where less imaginative people have left them for the trash collector. Little do they know what great cloches they make!

Materials and Tools
- Lampshade with metal frame
- Rust inhibitor
- Quick-drying latex primer
- Floater fabric
- Waxed dental floss or heavy string
- Scissors
- Paintbrush
- Large sewing needle
- Clothespins

Finding and Preparing the Perfect Lampshade Frame

⚜ Look for shades that are about 15 inches (38.1 cm) across and have metal frames. Some shades have no internal frame and gain their structural integrity with pleated sides. When you find this type, you can use it as it is, but don't expect it to last more than half a season before it self-destructs in the elements. Some shades are deceiving. They seem to have metal frames, but when their outer coverings are removed, the metal parts are in pieces and of no use. On the average, one out of every five lampshades I've found is perfect for cloches.

❧ Remove the existing cover from the lampshade with the scissors. When the covering's removed from a usable metal lampshade frame, you'll notice the junction points of the frame are soldered, and they clearly look like they'll stand up to some abuse. These will rust quite quickly when exposed to the elements, so protect the frame with a high-quality rust inhibitor that bonds with the rust and produces a hard surface that will take a coat of primer. A couple of coats of quick-drying latex primer give the extra protection needed to take the elements.

Sewing the Fabric to the Frame

❧ Cut rough pieces of floater fabric to fit around and on top of the frame. Attach them temporarily with clothespins. Use a big needle and waxed dental floss (which stands up well to inclement weather) to sew the fabric onto each structural piece of the frame. Because this fabric allows rain to penetrate, you can cover the top of the shade as well. When the shade's covered, it definitely looks like a nifty, old-time cloche. And the fabric deals with the two big challenges of cloche gardening by allowing hot air to get out and water to get in. You can also place a rock or brick on the bottom rim of the lampshade frame to secure it to the ground.

❧ If you don't have floater fabric, a less-perfect solution is to surround the frame with a double layer strip of 4-mil clear plastic. Attach the plastic to the frame with clear packing tape, and make sure you leave at least part of the top open to keep it from overheating.

If you aren't driven to scrounge for lampshade frames that work for you as cloches, you can make a similar cloche using something you may already have on hand.

TOMATO CAGE CLOCHE

If you turn the typical, store-bought tomato cage upside down and remove the three wire legs (or simply wrap the legs down around the rest of the cage), you'll find that it makes a great cloche frame. Wrap and sew these inverted tomato cage cloches with floater the same way you'd wrap the lampshade cloches. Tomato cages come in several diameters. You'll find that those with the largest top rings (averaging 15 inches [38.1 cm] in diameter) will be the best size for cloches. Since a tomato cage cloche is much taller than most available

A tomato cage cloche

cloches, you can use it to cover tomato plants in the spring and mature pepper plants in the fall. You may find that these frames are easier to cover with plastic than are the lampshade frame.

HOMEMADE PAPER HOT HATS

If you go to your local well-stocked garden center in the spring, chances are you'll find paper "hot caps" sold to cover plants right after you put them in the garden. These little season extension contraptions are about the size of a man's hat. They work great with warm-weather crops to give them a head start in the early spring. Though small, they're effective because they're not airtight and allow plenty of ventilation. They're held in place by mounding dirt around the base to cover tabs that are there for that purpose. They're kept in place for several weeks until the plants take hold and outgrow the caps. Of course, they seldom last more than one season and, hence, are inexpensive.

Given the life expectancy of hot caps, you may find it worthwhile to make up a bunch of similar hats from newspaper to place over your seedlings when they're transplanted into the garden in the spring. These are the typical Yankee-Doodle-Dandy affairs that you probably made yourself in kindergarten. It's a good way to get your kids occupied with a project on one of those snowy days in winter when schools are closed. Fifty of these homemade hot hats will take a couple of hours to make, and they'll definitely create a moderate environment to give your plants a jump start.

Here is how you make your own paper hot hats:
Take two newspaper pages (black and white only), and fold them together into a rectangle. Bring two opposite corners of the folded side together down the center to form a triangle. You'll be left with a long rectangle edge at the bottom. Roll up the long rectangular edge that remains at the bottom to form a brim. Open up the hat and place it over a plant. Load soil into the brim of the hat to keep it from blowing away. When the hat falls apart, send it to the compost pile.

There are several types of plastic hot caps made of recycled soft-drink bottles that will last through several seasons. Typically they're about 10 inches (25.4 cm) wide and 10 inches (25.4 cm) tall. They have tabs on the bottom to mound dirt to keep them in place, and they do a great job of protecting plants in the early spring. If you're thinking of buying these diminutive cloches, make sure they have adequate venting capacity through the top. The clear plastic will heat up inside very quickly on sunny days (regardless of outside temperatures) and can potentially do your plants more harm than good. I used these for several seasons on my tomatoes and peppers and ended up carefully cutting a hole in the tops the size of a tennis ball. This increased the contraption's ability to vent hot air freely without compromising the element of protection too severely.

WINDOW WELL COVER CLOCHES

Another cloche that can be manufactured at home is made from window well covers. These half-dome-shaped, hard plastic coverings are made to cover window wells of basement rooms to keep debris or water from getting into the window well, while still admitting light. You can usually find them at lumberyards or home centers. The first time I saw one of these used for season extension was at the home of a gardening acquaintance who had placed a window well cover against a brick wall on the south side of her house to force pots of spring daffodils. If you take two of these covers and place them back to back, you'll find that they create a plastic dome that provides up to 9 square feet (.8m²) of protected growing space. You can sandwich a piece of wood between the two well covers and screw them together. This will produce an excellent contraption for protecting lettuce and other cold-hardy salad crops in your garden. Leave gaps in the wood holding the two

well covers together to facilitate venting. The bottom edges of window well covers have horizontal lips that are big enough for bricks to sit on. Half a dozen bricks placed around the base of these contraptions will keep them in place. You can also create a simple frame you can attach the covers to.

CORRUGATED GREENHOUSE PLASTIC CLOCHE

Another cloche design that has great merit in the garden is a long, continuous design using a piece of corrugated greenhouse plastic. Simply bend the plastic into an upside-down "u" and place it over your plants. The ends are kept open for venting, and the long, narrow coverage is great for folks who garden in rows.

The Tiny Plot Propagation System

Reading about vintage growing systems that utilized cloches has allowed me to understand some basic concepts of cloche gardening that I've adapted to my garden. I use this time-tested system primarily to start cold-hardy plants, such as salad greens and brassicas. And it will allow you to grow stout and hardy transplant stock with a minimum amount of effort, in a small amount of space, and without the seed-starting mess in the kitchen that often accompanies cold-hardy plant propagation activities.

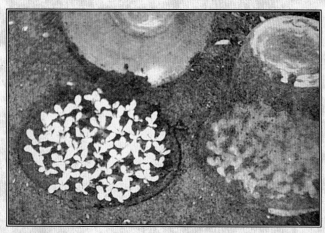

Lettuce seedlings started under glass cloches in a late-19th century market garden

The goal of this system is to get an early crop of cold-hardy transplants established that are acclimated to cold weather from the time of germination. In the early spring (before the last frosts have passed), this seed-starting system can be used as soon as the ground warms up inside the cloches (mid-February at my garden). You can also use it in midsummer to establish cold-hardy seedlings during the hot weather they don't enjoy. This system works well for any cold-hardy crop, but I use it most often for lettuce, kale, and broccoli, because those are crops my family relies on.

§ Begin by clearing out a 2 x 2-foot (61 x 61 cm) area. Mix in 2 inches (5.1 cm) of compost lightly into the soil, and smooth the soil out for seeding. Broadcast a full seed pack evenly across the area. Over this, sprinkle $^1/_4$ inch (6 mm) of seed-starting medium that contains perlite or vermiculite. This gives the new seedlings a weed-free environment in which to emerge.

§ Set a lampshade cloche in the middle of the seeded area; parts of the little plot that aren't covered by the cloche will still produce seedlings, though at a slower rate. If it's late July, and the transplants are for a fall crop, this tiny cloche-covered germination plot should be in the shade of something tall like okra or corn for part of the day, so the sun doesn't stress the tiny emerging seedlings. Though you shouldn't use a plastic-covered cloche in the summer (because they heat up too much), a floater-covered cloche moderates summertime temperatures and keeps the seedlings from drying out too quickly.

§ Two weeks after seedlings appear, give them a nice nutritional boost of fish emulsion mixed and dispensed from a watering can. As soon as the seedlings have their second set of leaves, cull plants in this seeded plot until the remaining baby plants are about 2 inches (5.1 cm) apart. Your first inclination will be to allow them to grow thickly and freely. You won't want to "waste" the little fellows by thinning. Be strong. Be brave. You must be ruthless in this thinning process to get the best transplants for the future. Old-timers used a method called "pricking" in which they lifted individual seedlings out by their roots and threw them away or transplanted them into rows. Though effective, the process is a bit tedious. If done properly, you can get 25 transplants from each plot. Care should be taken when pricking to disturb the soil as little as possible around the seedlings you're leaving behind; this is easier to do after a good rain, when the ground is more forgiving. A quicker way is to use sharp scissors to cut out unwanted seedlings at ground level, leaving their roots in the ground. Remember to replace the cloche after each thinning.

§ In about a month, your little propagation plot will be healthy and happy. Now it's time to transplant the seedlings to an area where the individual plants will mature. Prepare a new area for this crop in your garden. Water your propagation plot and allow time for the water to drain. Using a butter knife, cut lines between the seedlings so you'll be able use a small spatula or narrow garden trowel to lift seedlings out with a ball of soil. Transplant immediately to the area you've prepared. If possible, do this on an overcast day. Water sufficiently so the plants won't suffer too much shock, and have a piece of floater material on hand to cover your planted bed. If it's summer, spread a layer of hay or straw over the prepared soil before transplanting, so the weed-suppressing (and moisture-conserving) mulch is in place when you tuck these seedlings into their new home.

Old-time market gardeners protecting newly transplanted tomatoes under paper caps

No-Pain Cold Frames

IF YOU DON'T MAKE USE OF ANY OTHER season extension contraption (and you're a gardener who's serious enough about it to have a garden each year), you should have a cold frame somewhere on your property.

Turning Cold Frame Dreams into Reality

Chances are pretty good that you're a gardener of intermediate experience. Perhaps you've been tending a garden every summer for at least a couple of years, and you've done some reading about gardening. At some point along the way, you probably found yourself becoming mildly intrigued with the concept of season extension, or at least trying one of the many gardening techniques described in this book. Somehow, some way, right now, you probably have a couple of old windows somewhere around your home just waiting for the day when you'll build that cold frame you saw in someone's garden or on television. The window frames are probably in the garage leaning up against a wall behind some scrap pieces of wood. At the time, your mind was racing with thoughts of making the window sashes into a cold frame; but now they lean forlorn against the house, shielded by tall grass, with bottoms rotting.

The Many Ways to Use a Cold Frame

❧ Place plants that have been started indoors in a cold frame for several days to harden them off. This will lessen any transplant shock when they're placed in their new home in the garden bed.

❧ Force flower bulbs during the drab months of winter in a cold frame.

❧ You can avoid the typical seed-starting mess by starting seedlings in trays in a cold frame. The plants won't come up as quickly as they do under lights, but the stock will be sturdy, and they'll transplant well into the garden later.

❧ You can seed directly into the cold frame for later transplanting. You can also let the plants grow in the cold frame until harvest time. Salad greens do especially well growing in the fall and winter in cold frames.

❧ Instead of starting seeds in flats, you can reverse the order by starting your own and placing them at appropriate planting distances in the cold frame.

❧ Transplant biannuals into a cold frame in the fall. They'll give you a nice harvest the following spring before going to seed.

❧ You can overwinter tender or potted plants in a cold frame. Some gardeners produce their own slow-to-start perennials and shrubs from seeds or cuttings. When the first winter rolls around, those plants need an enhanced environment to spend the season, and a cold frame is perfect for this purpose.

❧ Just as warm-weather crops, such as tomato, squash, and okra, don't like cold weather, cold-hardy crops don't like hot weather. If you like lettuce, you can grow it in hot weather by making a cold frame sash that's covered with shade cloth.

❧ Some gardeners will load 3 inches (7.6 cm) of sand on top of plastic sheet bases inside of their cold frames to propagate perennial flowers and herbs from cuttings. The plastic keeps water from draining through to give cuttings a moist environment in which to root.

❧ In colder zones, you can grow tender crops in summer in a cold frame.

❧ If you want an early crop of the classic varieties of tomatoes, sweet corn, or many other tender crops, you can start seedlings in a cold frame two to five weeks before your last frost.

If your two window sashes are still in serviceable condition, I'm going to show you how to make them into a fine little cold frame that will allow you to harden off seedlings in the spring or grow some lettuce in the fall.

Cold Frame Basics

Before finally dusting off those old window frames and building your own cold frame, there are some factors to consider.

WINDOWS AS FRAMES

As I stated earlier, I never use glass for the top (also known as the "sash" or "light") of a cold frame. This goes against most of what one reads in gardening publications, and it's a disappointment to those of you who have old windows you want to use. The good news is, there are other materials that can be used to cover those sashes that give the gardener greater flexibility. So, you can still use those windows!

Since the fact remains that you still need a cold frame sash about the size of old windows, you can create a very appropriate cold frame cover by breaking the glass out of the windows and saving the frames. You should note that commercially available cold frames are often 2 x 4 feet (.6 x 1.2 m), but once you've begun using a frame of this size, you'll wish you had a larger one. A minimum size that will fit in a compact garden and give you a really serviceable season extension contraption is 3 x 6 feet (.9 x 1.8 m). Two 3 x 3-foot (.9 x .9 m) window frames work perfectly.

The Angle of the Sash

Peter Henderson, a leading market gardener during the middle to late 19th century, grew food year-round for folks living in New York City. He also wrote several books on the subject, including his classic, *Gardening for Profit* (Orange Judd Company, 1886). For his cold frames, Henderson (along with most other market gardeners of the time) used "simply two boards, running parallel, nailed to posts to secure them in line. The one in the back is 10 or 12 inches (25.4 or

You don't need to create an angle this steep to have an effective cold frame.

30.5 cm) wide, and that for the front 7 or 8 inches (17.8 or 20.3 cm), to give the sashes, when placed upon them, pitch enough to carry off the rain, and to better catch the sun's rays." A lot has been written about the proper angle for the top of the sash to absorb the maximum amount of light. Some books and articles will have you believe that at more northerly locations, one must build a cold frame with a high back and a steeply angled frame top. Old-time market gardeners kept it simple. They grew fruit and vegetables productively in their low-pitched frames for hundreds of years.

The point to be considered here is that, though similar in many respects, cold frames are not greenhouses. The carefully calculated angles on the south sides of conventional home-attached greenhouses and sun spaces are required to maximize light penetration by low midwinter sun angles. The steep angles seen and recommended on the sashes of some cold frames aren't necessary to have a frame that will produce. What's important is that you maximize available light. Old-time market gardeners used sashes that were 6 x 6 feet (1.8 x 1.8 m). This size gave a lot of protected space for growing crops, but that extra width on the frame allowed even the low angle of the winter sun to flood the frame.

Later on in this chapter, I'll show you how to make an effective cold frame that's designed to be 5 feet (1.5 m) wide. But you can increase the available light in a smaller-sized cold frame by painting the inside of the contraption white to reflect and maximize available light.

Creating a Traditional Cold Frame

At the front end of this discussion, it's worth noting that you can set your window panes on top of four bales of straw arranged in a rectangular configuration. This will create a serviceable, enhanced growing environment that you can assemble in a few minutes. For a more permanent cold frame, use the following instructions. Readjust your cut list dimensions according to the size of your window frames.

Materials and Tools List for the 3 x 6-foot (.9 x 1.8 m) Cold Frame

- 2 window frames, with glass removed
- 1 piece of untreated 2 x 12 hemlock framing lumber, 12 feet (3.6 m) long
- 1 piece of untreated 2 x 8 hemlock framing lumber, 8 feet (2.4 m) long
- One tube exterior construction glue
- #16 galvanized ring shank nails
- 8 L-shaped plates
- White primer (optional)
- Fencing (optional)
- Fence staples (optional)
- 10 x 25-foot (3 x 7.5 m) package of clear 4-mil plastic
- 4 galvanized hinges

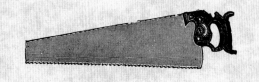

- 2 hooks and eyes
- Tape measure
- Saw
- Drill
- Hammer
- Screwdriver
- Paintbrush (optional)
- Wire cutters (optional)
- Scissors
- Stapler

Cut List

CODE	DESCRIPTION	QTY.	MATERIAL	DIMENSIONS
A	Sash	2	old windows	36 x 36" (91.4 x 91.4 cm)
B	Front	1	2 x 8	72" (182.8 cm) long
C	Back	1	2 x 12	72" (182.8 cm) long
D	Sides★	2	2 x 12	33" (83.8 cm)

★ These two side pieces are ripped so one edge tapers from 8 inches (20.3 cm) to the full 12-inch (30.5 cm) width. This length is determined by taking the width of the sash and subtracting the thickness of the front and the back pieces of framing lumber (which in this case is 3 inches [7.6 cm]).

Assembly of the Frame

Predrill five $^1/_8$-inch (3 mm) holes at each end of the front (B) and back (C) pieces, $^3/_4$ inch (1.9 cm) from the edges. On a large flat surface, set up parts B, C, and D. Glue and nail the box together, and make sure all the bottoms of the boards are sitting flat on the ground. When assembled, turn the unit upside down so the cut edges of the sides are facing down. You now have a flat-top surface for the sash to sit on, and the frame is angled slightly. Before the glue has dried, take diagonal measurements and adjust the frame until the measurements are the same to ensure the frame is square (see page 27).

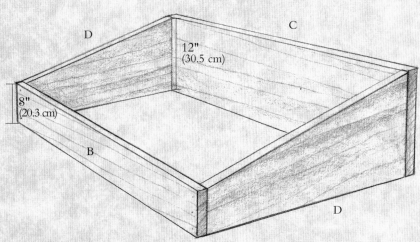

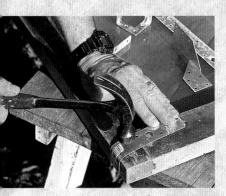

Note that the framing strap is being placed on the window before the glass is removed (and while the window still has structural integrity).

⚶ Regardless of the size of the sashes you've chosen, the measurements of the front and back pieces are always as long as the total width of the two (or more) sashes you've chosen. And the two tapered sides are always the width of the sash, minus the combined thickness of the front and rear sash (which, in this project, is 3 inches [7.6 cm]).

Sash Assembly

⚶ An old window frame will sometimes seem more flimsy when the glass has been removed. If this is the case, purchase L-shaped plates (they come with screws) and install them on the corners of the frame to reinforce it. You can also purchase framing plates and wrap the corners with them, securing through the provided holes with #8 Phillips-head, pan-style screws. (Before installing plates, make sure the sash is square by taking diagonal measurements [see page 27].)

Painting

⚶ This step isn't absolutely necessary unless you want to seal in old paint on window sashes that you fear may contain lead. I paint the sashes and the inside of the frame with white primer because white is far superior to either silver or

This 5 x 10-foot (1.5 x 3 m) frame has been set up specifically for growing seedlings and overwintering potted plants. There's no soil in this frame for growing plants to maturity. The interior was painted white in order to increase reflected light, while the dark-colored gravel was used to absorb heat (as well as to drain water).

black for interior surfaces. As I said before, a coat of white primer increases reflected light inside the frame. Black remains the best color for absorbing heat if your frame has stone or water storage at the rear of the frame. There's also a type of foil-faced rigid insulation that reflects a lot of heat back into the frame. But the intention here in painting is to reflect light, and painting the inside white is the best way to achieve that.

Fencing the Sashes

▨ To add structural integrity to the plastic sash covering you may wish to add two pieces of fencing to cover each sash. Secure them to the sashes with fence staples. I've used chicken wire for this purpose and have found it to be a bit frustrating to work with because it has little wire spurs that get caught on tender skin. I've also used standard galvanized fencing that has 2 x 4-inch (5.1 x 10.2 cm) openings and have found that it does a great job in supporting plastic or floater if you decide to cover the sashes with either of those materials. When you cut the fencing, measure the pieces 1 inch (2.5 cm) shorter so they won't hang over the edges. I mention the use of fencing because it does support flexible coverings, especially with heavy snow loads, but it isn't absolutely necessary if you do a good job in wrapping and stapling the plastic onto the sash frame.

Covering and Attaching the Sash

▨ Wrap the sash in three layers of 4-mil plastic, and you'll have a 12-mil covering with dead airspace to act as insulation. Staple the plastic to the sash, and tuck in the corners to make it look pretty.

▨ Use the four galvanized hinges for the two sashes, and attach the sashes to the back of the frame with them. Put a couple of hooks and eyes at the front edge to keep the sash in place during windy conditions, and you're set to go.

A hinge bent around a window frame on a 3 x 6-foot (.9 x 1.8 m) cold frame

Creating a High-Performance Cold Frame

A 3 x 6-foot (.9 x 1.8 m) cold frame is about as small a contraption a home gardener should make. It's worth mentioning that an excellent sash can be made from a screen door frame that would produce a cold frame about 3 x 6½ feet (.9 x 2 m). This humble size has kept many gardeners happy, but you can put together a custom cold frame that more completely anticipates your gardening needs in size and design.

Once you've assembled your first 3 x 6-foot (.9 x 1.8 m) cold frame, you'll find that it's a lot handier than you ever would have imagined. Furthermore, I'd bet a dollar to a doughnut that you'll wish you had built a bigger contraption before the first anniversary of its creation rolls around. If you're going to do the work of building a cold frame, *and* you have the room to put it in your yard or garden (this being the most important point), you should really consider making a larger frame.

The design that you're about to look at is 5 x 10 feet (1.5 x 3 m). It seems only slightly bigger than the 3 x 6-foot (.9 x 1.8 m) frame when placed side by side, but the larger frame offers significantly greater flexibility because of the additional 32 square feet (3 m²) of space. This is the size of my current cold frame, and I've found it to be a serviceable size. This design also incorporates a practical, low-cost design feature, which allows for venting when you aren't home.

Materials and Tools List for the 5 x 10-foot (1.5 x 3 m) Cold Frame

- 2 pieces 2 x 12 framing lumber (pine, hemlock, redwood, or cedar), 10 feet (3 m) long
- 1 piece 2 x 8 framing lumber, 10 feet (3 m) long
- One tube exterior construction glue
- #16 galvanized ring shank nails

- Tape measure
- Saw
- Drill
- Hammer

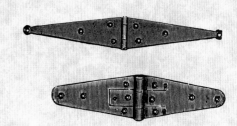

Cut List

CODE	DESCRIPTION	QTY.	MATERIAL	DIMENSIONS
A	(see Designing and Manufacturing a Custom Sash Frame)			
B	Front	1	2 x 8	120" (304.8 cm) long
C	Back	1	2 x 12	120" (304.8 cm) long
D	Sides	2	2 x 12	57" (142.5 cm) long, tapered lengthwise from full width to $7^1/_2$" (19.1 cm)

Assembly of Frame

Follow assembly instructions on page 65.

DESIGNING AND MANUFACTURING A CUSTOM SASH FRAME WITH VENT

The following method of sash frame assembly was developed from systems that co-workers and I have used for creating a protected environment around vintage homes during exterior renovations in winter months. Basically, we made frames from low-cost 1 x 3 lumber (sometimes called furring or strapping) that was held together at the corners with $1^1/_4$-inch (3.2 cm) plasterboard screws. The frames were then covered with clear, 6-mil construction-grade plastic and stapled to the frame. They were lightweight and created a working environment that was wind-free and that warmed up by as much as 30°F (17°C) when the sun came out.

When I started making various season extenders, I used this same technique to create sashes for my cold frames. Though there were minor design improvements to be made when these panels were used in the garden, my biggest challenge with them was to create an inexpensive system of assembly that didn't require half-lapping or mitering connection points. They also needed to maintain structural integrity and look good. What I came up with is simple and will stand up to a lot of abuse.

Materials for the Sash with Vent for the 5 x 10-foot (1.5 x 3 m) Cold Frame

- 7 pieces 1 x 4 pine board, 120 inches (304.8 cm) long
- 18 framing plates, 1 x 12 inches (2.5 x 30.5 cm), bent (see page 26)
- #8, Phillips-head, pan-style screws
- 2 galvanized "T" hinges, 3 inches (7.6 cm)
- 2 galvanized "T" hinges, 4 inches (10.2 cm)
- Lag bolts, to attach hinges from sash to frame
- Nuts and bolts, to attach hinges from vent to sash

Cut List★

Code	Qty.	Material	Dimensions
E	2	1 x 4	120" (304.8 cm) long
F	4	1 x 4	53" (134.6 cm) long
G	1	1 x 4	60" (152.4 cm) long
H	2	1 x 4	35" (88.9 cm) long
I	2	1 x 4	14$^{1}/_{2}$" (36.8 cm) long
J	2	1 x 4	67" (170.2 cm) long

★ Make sure you mark each piece with the letter designation as you cut it so you aren't confused by various pieces of scrap that will be left over after the stock has been cut.

Constructing the Vented Sash

▧ The sash frame is designed in a manner that will allow you to create panels of any size for future season extension systems you may desire. You can easily adapt this design to create two separate sashes with vents. Each junction of two pieces is held together with bent framing plates.

▧ Place pieces E through J on a hard, flat surface according to figure 2. Dimensions may vary slightly depending on the actual thickness of your 1 x 4s. These are based on an average width of 3$^{1}/_{2}$ inches (8.9 cm). Bend the plates (see page 26).

▧ Mark the location spots on all pieces of both the vent frame and sash frame, as indicated with stars in figure 2. Attach the framing plates securely to both sides of each piece with the screws.

▧ Butt intersecting pieces, and make sure the framing plates sandwich the intersecting 1 x 4s. Attach each intersecting piece with one screw per plate. (Don't attach with more than one screw per plate at this time.) Take diagonal meas-

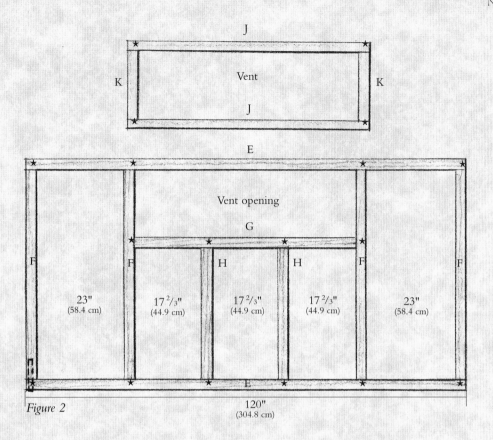

Figure 2

urements to make sure the frames are square (see page 27). Then complete attaching all the perpendicular pieces with screws on both sides.

5 If you want to add a piece of fencing to increase structural integrity, you should do it at this point. You can run the fence over the vent opening, even though the opening won't be covered with the same covering as the sash.

§ Cover the sash frame with 6-mil, UV-resistant greenhouse plastic. When covering the frame, make sure that you leave the vent hole open by cutting an "X" through the space and folding the edges under and stapling them securely.

§ You can cover the vent frame with the same plastic you used to cover the rest of the sash, or use floater material instead. Read the section on page 75 on Venting Your Frame for more information.

§ Attach the vent frame to the sash frame with the 3-inch (7.6 cm) hinges. Attach the sash to the cold frame base with the 4-inch (10.2 cm) hinges.

Cold Frame Considerations

Once the sash or sashes are attached to the frame, you have a very serviceable cold frame that can be moved to different areas in your garden quite easily.

MICROCLIMATES IN BIGGER COLD FRAMES

Jumbo-sized cold frames, when insulated around the base to keep out the cold, will create distinct microclimates inside the frame. The upper left corner of a south-facing frame is always the hottest corner and is the first spot that you should put your most tender plants. During two separate spring seasons, I've grown miniature determinate varieties of tomato in a high-topped, 4 x 12-foot (1.6 x 3.6 m) cold frame, beginning eight weeks before the last frost in Zone 5 Rhode Island. There's no question that the individual tomato plants in the upper left corner of the cold frame fared significantly better than tomatoes in

oother parts of the frame. That's a good indication of the differences in growing conditions that are available inside even the relatively small area of a cold frame.

SASH OPTIONS FOR EVEN BIGGER COLD FRAMES

If you plan to make a cold frame bigger than 5 x 10-foot (1.5 x 3 m), it's advisable to create two or three sashes to cover it so you aren't dealing with a single, large, unwieldy wind catcher. There's another reason, besides the potential unwieldiness of one large sash, why you may wish to put two sashes on your cold frame. A plastic-covered sash will create a warmer environment, while a floater-covered sash will allow for penetration of moisture by rain and snow. With both coverings on the same double-sashed frame, you have the further flexibility of creating two even more distinct microclimates within the same contraption.

PLACEMENT OF THE COLD FRAME

A lot of folks put their cold frames in their gardens. And it does make sense to put them there because that's where the gardening happens. But there will be times when the only gardening that's going on in your garden will be in your cold frame. I know some darn good gardeners who use only a cold frame outside the normal growing season. They never mess with any of the other contraptions that I talk about in this book. Most of the cold frames used by this type of gardener are placed on the south side of the house. Placing a cold frame with its back against a south-facing wall of your house makes a lot of sense. It's guaranteed to be warmer than if it's in the garden where it sits alone and exposed to the elements. It's also much easier to check on your cold frame as you're coming in and out of the house. My own frame sits about five steps from my back door, and I know for certain that I check it more often than if it sat in my garden, 40 steps farther away. If you're concerned about lead in the soil around your house (from peeled and scraped lead-based paint), you can excavate the soil and replace it with soil you know is uncontaminated.

Permanently Installing Your Cold Frame

❦ Choose a site that receives sun exposure all day. Set the frame on the site. Close the sash to make sure the frame is square; if not, simply push one side of the frame into position until it lines up with the sash.

❦ Mark a line 2 inches (5.1 cm) beyond the outside of the frame. Remove the frame and excavate the area approximately 5 inches (12.7 cm) to create a level, sunken platform. Place the cold frame into the sunken area. Use a level on the back and front of the cold frame to make sure it's sitting exactly level; if it's not, use a shovel to excavate the area that's keeping the frame from sitting level. Close the sash again to make sure the frame's sitting square, and adjust accordingly.

❦ Drive a 3-foot (.9 m) rebar stake into the ground inside each corner. Once they're driven below the top of the frame, drive four 1¹⁄₄-inch (3.2 cm) fence staples into the corners around the rebar to secure the cold frame. Once the rebar stakes have been attached to the inside of the frame, it's in a secure position and you'll be able to insulate the exterior if you desire.

Insulating the Frame

Some gardening books that discuss cold frames often talk about making sashes tight to keep the cold out. I'm of a different opinion. From my own experience, more harm is done to plants inside a cold frame because of overheating, than is done by allowing the plants to get frosted ears when I've erred on the side of too much venting. Designing a dependable system that allows for hot air to escape is the key to helping your plants in cold months. If it gets bitter enough to hurt the plants on a cold night, you'll need to cover the cold frame with a blanket or tarp anyway. Charles Nissley, in *Starting Early Vegetable and Flowering Plants Under Glass* (Orange Judd Company,1929), described market gardeners in New Jersey starting cauliflower seedlings in cold frames in midwinter. Those gardeners closed the sashes only on the most extreme days to ensure that the seedlings that emerged were healthy, strong, and well acclimated to Zone–5 weather. And vintage photos of numerous late 19th century cold frames show coverings made of rye straw mats to maintain heat inside frames when temperatures turned bitter.

Though plants do very well with plenty of airflow around their heads, they do benefit from having warm feet inside a cold frame. After you set your cold frame in a south-facing location in your garden, you should bank soil around the outside of the frame to moderate inside soil temperatures. If you want to go the extra mile in securing more moderate soil temperatures inside the frame, excavate a trench on the outside of the frame when you're excavating the inside. (At this point, your frame will be suspended from the four corners by the rebar stakes, and you'll be able to excavate around the suspended frame.) Slide pieces of 2-inch-thick (5.1 cm) rigid insulation into the trench and up the sides of the wood frame and cover it with banked soil.

Rye straw mats covering cold frames for protection against cold weather

VENTING YOUR FRAME

One sunny February morning after a night of snow in the early 1990s, I called up Paul Ladd of Wakefield, Rhode Island, to arrange a time to go see his cold frame. He invited me right over. When we walked out onto the south side of his house, I could see that he had already been busy shoveling snow off the top of his 6 x 15-foot (1.8 x 4.5 cm) frame. Although the temperature was still below freezing, condensation was already forming on the underside of the sashes from the accumulating heat inside the frame. As we were chatting, Paul walked over to a snow-covered pile of something and pulled out two blocks of wood. He walked casually over to the cold frame and slipped the blocks under two of the five sashes on the frame to allow some of the accumulating hot air to escape. It was clearly something he had done countless times before. People who heat with a wood-burning stove have a special relationship with their stove; by winter's end a wood stove aficionado knows exactly what it takes to make his or her stove function to its greatest potential. It was clear to me that Paul had developed a similar intimate relationship with his cold frame. On that cold and sunny morning, Paul knew what he had to do to allow his cold frame to vent properly for the given temperature and sun exposure of the moment. Paul had built his cold frame (a simple box of 2 x 12 redwood sitting on the ground, covered with five old-time cypress sashes that he had purchased in 1947) for the sole purpose of growing lettuce in the winter. I'm certain that after more than 50 years of using the same frame, he made the appropriate daily (and as often as needed when he was at home) venting adjustments on his frame without even thinking about it.

Paul Ladd's cold frame

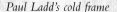

When I first met Paul, he had been retired for some time and could keep an eye on his frame, but I don't know what he did when he was younger and busy raising 11 children with his wife. In an ideal world, you would never leave your garden, being always on hand to open your frame on hot days and to close it again when the temperature drops. But hectic schedules in a busy society may mean that you must neglect your frame for several days at a time. Most other cold frames that you see will need to be vented by lifting up the whole sash. This venting method leaves much to be desired because it exposes everything inside the frame to bitter cold if you're gone for a time when the weather changes.

The high-performance cold frame sash on page 67 is set up with a vent at the top of the sash that allows you to leave it open on cold mornings when you go to work. This detail allows you to vent the frame without opening the entire sash. Or if you're covering a cold frame sash with rigid plastic or greenhouse film, you can cover the vent frame with floater. Such a covering over the vent allows hot air to escape while you're at work. And it'll still have the protective covering of the fabric when it cools down later in the afternoon.

Automatic Vent Openers

Purchased automatic vent openers are a swell addition to a cold frame, if you can get them to work dependably. Generally, automatic openers are attached to the front of the sash and rest inside. As the interior of the cold frame heats up, the gas inside the main cylinder of the vent opener expands and drives a rod out to open up the sash. As the air cools around the cylinder of the opener, the gas inside it cools, allowing the rod to retreat into the cylinder, closing the sash. Unfortunately, these clever gizmos seldom actually lift even two-thirds of the weight that the

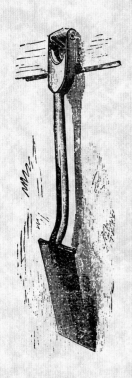

manufacturers suggest. The problem is that the weight of the sash is often right on the border of the maximum weight that an opener can handle.

To tell how heavy the sash or sash vent is so you know what your automatic opener will need to lift, first attach the sash or sash vent to the back of the frame to get an accurate reading. Then, slide a common bathroom scale under the front of the sash so that the sash rests on the scale. With the weight readings on the outside of the frame where you can see it, lift the scale (with the sash riding on it) and the weight of the sash will register on the scale. One of the slick benefits of the high-performance sash design is that the built-in vent door is considerably lighter than the sash itself and an automatic vent opener will perform very well with it.

But it isn't necessary to install an automatic vent opener on a cold frame to make it highly functional. Old-time market gardeners used blocks of wood with notches cut in them to allow different venting heights on the sashes. You can do the same, but a more secure method is to purchase pairs of hooks and eyes of different lengths (3, 6, and 10 inches [7.6, 15.2, and 25.4 cm]) to install on the front corners of your cold frame's sash and sash vent. This allows you to keep the sash and/or vent open securely at different heights. You can also keep the sash and vent closed tightly with the same hooks. If you look around, you can find hook and eye combinations that have spring-loaded locking devices that keep the hooks secured on the eyes.

SETTING UP THE INTERIOR OF YOUR COLD FRAME FOR GREAT RESULTS

To get an outstanding installation, excavate the soil inside your frame 12 to 16 inches (30.5 to 40.6 cm) below the outside grade. The purpose of this is threefold. First, it allows you to manipulate your soil mixture. Second, it gives plants greater headroom when the soil mixture is added back in. Finally, it creates plenty of room for drainage in case water enters the frame from a downpour when the ground outside the frame is frozen. As you excavate, save the soil to one side onto a tarp for later use. You'll immediately see the benefit of securing the frame at the corners with rebar, from which the box of the frame will hang as you're excavating.

To create a proper base for draining your soil, it's a great idea to load 4 inches (10.2 cm) of gravel in the bottom, and then to cover it with $1/2$-inch

(1.3 cm) hardware cloth to keep the soil separated from the gravel. If you expect to only grow plants directly in the soil, you can fill in with 8 inches (20.3 cm) of compost-amended topsoil for growing lettuce and cold-hardy greens. Some gardeners get greater flexibility out of their cold frames by keeping portions of them in gravel to force bulbs in pots and start of seedlings in flats or trays. It's also a great idea to lay a 2 x 6 piece of lumber every 3 feet (.9 m) (running front to back) on the soil-filled portion to allow a place to stand inside the frame so the soil doesn't get compacted. If you build one frame, I suggest you make one-quarter to one-third of it into a forcing and seeded tray area with a gravel bottom, and the rest into a planting area that has a rich soil mixture. By placing a permanent gravel bottom for the seeded tray area, you'll have a weed-free area that drains well when you're watering seed trays of emerging seedlings that'll be placed in the garden later.

Making Rocket-Fuel Soil

§ Once you've excavated the soil inside the frame, you should have a pile of saved soil to one side. Look at the quality of the soil you've excavated with a critical eye toward improving it. Add a 25-pound (11.4 kg) bag of composted cow manure and 20 pounds (9 kg) of soil-less seed-starting medium (that contains a lot of perlite or vermiculite to lighten your soil). Then add 1 cup (224 g) each of greensand, rock phosphate, and lime—all important organic amendments to give your soil the necessary trace elements to produce high-performance results. Thoroughly mix all the amendments up with the excavated soil.

§ It goes without saying that you want to remove any weed roots and large stones that may be lurking in the soil. Take into consideration that you want really outstanding soil in your cold frame, probably better than what you have in your garden as a whole. You can substitute compost for the bagged composted cow manure. If you're unsatisfied with the look and feel of the soil, add more compost. Return enough of the mix to the inside of the frame to give you 8 inches (20.3 cm) of high-quality planting soil. Eight inches (20.3 cm) of soil will leave the planting surface several inches below the outside grade; this will allow for more headroom for your plants.

Early settlers in the American Great Plains used sunken cold frames like these to grow tender crops.

Keeping the Weeds at Bay

If you're planning on not using your cold frame for a time, or there are sections of the frame you aren't using, you can take steps to keep weeds from germinating in the unused areas.

🌢 Cultivate the soil lightly and rake it smooth. Spread a $\frac{1}{2}$-inch-thick (1.3 cm) layer of wet newspaper (keep out the color sections) over the area not in use. The layer of wet newspaper will dry into an organic mat that will suppress weed germination. Freshly cultivated soil will be ready for you to plant (with a minimum amount of reworking) when you remove the mulch mat. You can do the same with a big piece of cardboard. The benefit of using wet newspaper, however, is that you can achieve a very tight bond on the inside edges of the frame, though cardboard will do an adequate job.

I'm no prophet, but I predict you won't use this newspaper mat strategy until you have, at least once, allowed weeds to take over your frame during a time when you're too busy to use it. All it takes for a gardener to remember to always take steps to suppress weeds in an unused cold frame is to let him or her go through the senseless hard work of removing weeds, many of which have rushed to seed in the enhanced growing environment of the cold frame. If weeds have seeded, and spread their future offspring onto the surface of your frame before you wake up and remove them, your next plants will have a heck of a time competing with the weeds.

Here's a simple variation of a cold frame sash with a vent. An automatic vent opener keeps the vent open when heat accumulates inside the frame.

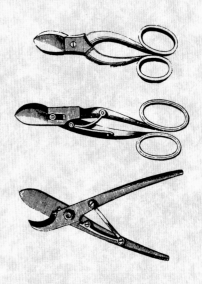

If you find the growing surface of your cold frame has acquired a layer of weed seeds, you can kill the weed seeds organically with a process known as "solarization." To accomplish this, suppress any more growth with the newspaper mulch mat. When the weather is midsummer hot, take off the mulch mat and water the surface thoroughly. Immediately cover the whole frame with two layers of clear 4-mil plastic. Hold the edges of the plastic down around the outside edges of the cold frame with rocks and leave it there for four weeks. This allows inside soil temperatures to soar high enough to kill weed seeds.

When you open your frame back up after this process, it will be filled with newly sterilized soil. While it has killed off the weed seeds, the solarization process has also knocked out all the microorganisms, which are so important for healthy soil. You can reinoculate your cold frame soil with a shovel full of healthy garden soil or compost that's guaranteed to have gazillions of those beneficial microcreatures.

Overwintering in Cold Frames

One strategy that market gardeners used to get early crops in the spring was to overwinter plants in cold frames. In Zone 5 of the New York City area, Peter Henderson sowed seeds of Early Jersey Wakefield cabbage, cauliflower, and lettuce on September 15. Planting earlier than this caused the plants to run to seed. A month later, he transplanted the seedlings into cold frames for the winter. Henderson packed seedlings into frames for overwintering at a rate of 500 cabbage or cauliflower plants, or 800 lettuce plants for every 3 x 6-foot (.9 x

Instead of transplanting your cold frame seedlings, you can let them grow right where they are.

1.8 m) sash. He called these seedlings "almost hardy" and able to withstand "severe freezing without injury." He also made it clear that these fall planted veggies should be "treated as their nature demands; that is, after transplanting the cabbage, lettuce, or cauliflower into frames (which, will be about the middle or end of October), the sashes need not be put on for a month or six weeks after, unless a very cold spell comes for a day or two."

Henderson went on to say, "Even on clear winter days, when the thermometer marks fifteen or twenty degrees (-9° or -7°C) in the shade, they must be abundantly aired." This seems like rough treatment for plants, but it kept the seedlings from going to seed, and it created extremely hardy plants that could take the cold of the winter months ahead. Henderson used only the cover of glass sashes to protect cabbage and lettuce during cold snaps and added a cov-

The Five Rules of Thumb for Effective Use of Cold Frames

🌿 **Wetter Ain't Better:** Soak the soil inside your frame thoroughly, and then allow it to become nearly dry to encourage deep root development. When plants need it, water early in the day to discourage dampening off in growing seedlings or transplants.

🌿 **Don't Be Mean…Lean:** The plants inside your frame won't appreciate ground-compacting footsteps. Do your work by leaning over the edge of the frame or install permanent stepping boards to stand on when you're working the frame from the inside.

🌿 **Survive a Freeze, You'll Be Pleased:** If it's cold enough to even think about throwing an extra blanket on your bed at night, then you should throw an old carpet over the top of your cold frame to retain heat.

🌿 **High/Low Will Really Show:** To get finely tuned to the nuances of the performance of your frame, purchase a high/low thermometer and place it inside for easy monitoring.

🌿 **Eat in Season, There's a Reason:** Use your cold frame to increase the harvest periods of in-season veggies and flowers rather than attempting to force plants that would grow in radically different temperatures. Your goal is to assist nature, not dominate it.

ering of rye straw mats to protect the less-hardy cauliflower when temperatures dropped below 5°F (-15°C).

In late February, the lettuce seedlings were transplanted into other cold frames that had been filled with leaves and covered with sashes all winter, keeping the soil warm through the cold months. Plants were now spaced about 8 inches (20.3 cm) apart and covered with sashes at night and during cold days. Sashes were opened on warm days and when it rained. This forced the hardened lettuce into a growing spurt, making lettuce ready for market in six weeks.

Once the lettuce was harvested in mid-May, Henderson planted five or six cucumber seeds (he grew Improved White Spine Cucumber) in the center of each frame. Sashes were left in place until the cucumbers began to be sold in mid-June.

The cabbage and cauliflower seedlings were transplanted once again, this time from the frames into fields in late March or early April. They were ready for market by early summer. At that point, a planting of celery was made, which was ready for harvest by fall, when cabbage, lettuce, and cauliflower were sown for the purpose of beginning this high-performance cycle once again.

Henderson maintained that this was a very commonly used strategy by commercial gardeners of his time. In his own operations, he produced "several hundred thousands of fall sown plants annually." He also pointed out that with this system, the same frames were used three times per season.

WHAT CAN WE LEARN FROM VINTAGE OVERWINTERING STRATEGIES?

There are a few points for modern home gardeners to consider in this system. The first thing to notice is that these old-timers spent a lot of effort in transplanting hundreds of thousands of seedlings and overwintered starts. Once I

Old-time cloth-covered frames

These two vintage photographs show old-time methods of crop irrigation.

realized that seedlings and young plants could take the inevitable transplant shock without an appreciable amount of harm, I adopted the same attitude of aggressive transplanting. The goal in a highly productive garden, with excellent soil fertility, is to transplant younger plants immediately into holes left open by harvest. Regardless of the season, you should have small plots of seedlings growing to transplant into the openings. Transplant shock will be lessened if it's done on an overcast day and enough soil is taken with the seedling to not stress the roots. You should do it quickly and water-in well with gentle showers from a hose or watering bucket.

Home gardeners don't need hundreds of thousands of plants, but they can make use of 20 plants sown biweekly. Henderson even believed that the freezing and thawing of seedlings in winter cold frames was "necessary for their safety" in cold weather. He typically lost about 2 percent of his winter seedlings. It's hard to argue with his several decades of success in Zone 5. And finally, once again, we see that cold-hardy plants (and especially young plants) are pretty darn rugged in their ability to withstand the cold if they're given even a small amount of protection.

Forcing Bulbs in a Cold Frame

HERE IS A METHOD FOR FORCING TULIPS, DAFFODILS, IRISES, and paperwhites in a cold frame:

❧ The time to start the process is in the fall, and the best containers for forcing are shallow pots made for that purpose. The free alternative is plastic plant pots, which can be acquired fairly easily by asking landscapers for their used containers.

❧ To create a proper potting mix, combine equal parts of potting soil, perlite, and peat moss. Then mix two parts of this combination with one part coarse sand. Fill your pots two-thirds of the way with the soil mixture and crowd the bulbs in to ensure a strong showing. Set the bulbs with the pointed side up, and leave $1/4$ inch (6 mm) between each bulb. Tulip bulbs usually have a flat side: place these flat sides to the outside to concentrate the blooming stems to the center of the pot. Daffodils and miniature irises can be set in two layers, with the round bottoms of the upper bulbs nestled between the pointed necks of the lower bulbs to make for spectacular displays. Each pot should have a minimum of five bulbs. Cover with more of your potting mix, leaving the tops just barely visible. Water thoroughly to settle the soil, and add more of the mix as needed.

❧ Your goal is to manipulate the life cycle of these flowering plants so you can get a show of emerging blossoms when you want them. You'll need several weeks of cool, fall weather with daytime temperatures in the mid-fifties (in the teens for Celsius) to get roots established before freezing temperatures set in. Tulips need 16 to 18 weeks of cold (including the cool fall weeks); daffodils need 17 to 19 weeks, and small bulbs such as crocuses and miniature irises need about 12 weeks.

❧ During the winter, keep the pots of bulbs in a shady, unheated space where mice can't get to them. I keep mine on the north side of the garden shed under $1/2$-inch (1.3 cm) hardware cloth and a protective loose layer of hay or straw. Two to four weeks before you want to display them, raise temperatures to no more than 55°F (13°C) to begin the forcing process by placing them in your frame. An extra covering of blankets and old tarps will keep them warm when temperatures drop at night.

❧ Once unopened flowerbuds appear, bring the pot inside for display.

❧ Keep track of how long it takes for the bulbs to emerge from their winter slumber in your frame. Some colder regions may take longer than others, but your bulbs will emerge all the same. Set up half a dozen pots and stagger their placement in your cold frame every week, beginning in midwinter to ensure a steady supply of spring color.

THE ULTIMATE GREENHOUSE

FOR MANY YEARS, I BUILT AND USED COLD FRAMES, tunnels, and stoop houses, but I never built a greenhouse for myself. I've coordinated season extension courses for small-time farmers at our local technical college that included speakers who use greenhouses very effectively for a variety of tasks, but I never built a greenhouse for myself. I built greenhouses for others, but I never built one for myself. I have gone out of my way to look carefully at various greenhouses, both their construction and use, but in all this time, I never got around to building one for my own garden. So, by the time I got around to building a greenhouse for my own family, I knew exactly what I wanted.

In terms of construction, I wanted to build a hoop-style, plastic-covered greenhouse, with components that would cost less than kits. In terms of use, I wanted to be able to grow cold-hardy veggies and salad greens in permanent beds through the winter. I also wanted to be able to get an early start on warm-weather crops so they could be harvested significantly earlier than normal. And I wanted one of the growing beds to have the capacity for a double covering that would be simple to deal with. Fortunately for me, I didn't need to reinvent the wheel to get what I wanted.

Many Ways to Use a Greenhouse

§ With your greenhouse, you'll create an indoor garden that stays warm all-year round and provides you with as many possibilities as you can think up.

§ You can grow cold-hardy greens throughout the winter.

§ You can get an early start on your peas and other warm-weather crops.

§ Your tomatoes can grow in a blight-free environment.

§ In colder zones, you can grow melons and other tender crops.

§ You can manipulate layers very effectively to anticipate any weather condition.

Greenhouse Basics

When it comes to owner-assembled garden greenhouses, a phenomenon has taken place over the last 25 years. At some point in season extension history, gardeners all over the country saw the value of using PVC plumbing pipe for the structure of plastic-covered greenhouses. By a simple process of elimination, most owner-made hoop greenhouses have the same design features, because the same components are available everywhere, and they fulfill the need for the least amount of money. Though I'm sure people around the country were talking amongst themselves about the construction method I'll be describing, a mass of these similar structures sprouted up around the world in a relatively simultaneous manner, without a serious amount of interaction between the builders.

On the two sides of the greenhouse, 5-foot (1.5 m) sections of $1^1/_4$-inch (3.2 cm) metal electric conduit pipe (also known as EMT) are driven halfway into the ground. Twenty-foot (6 m) lengths of $1^1/_2$-inch (3.8 cm) PVC pipe are then slipped over the tops of the EMT pipes to create a Quonset-style structure. The ends are framed with wood, and the whole structure is covered with plastic. A greenhouse using 20-foot-long (6 m) pipe for hoops results in a greenhouse about 14 feet (4.2 m) wide. Venting is then installed in various ways to accommodate the specific use and gardening zone of the owner.

There are slight variations on the materials for this structure and the materials used. Sometimes, folks use EMT for the hoops and embed the ends in concrete. These greenhouses are usually only 10 feet (3 m) wide. Some folks place rebar inside 20-foot (6 m) lengths of PVC pipe for reinforcement and end up with a greenhouse about 12 feet (3.6 m) wide.

At this point this greenhouse may not sound much different from the stoop house. Two people can assemble a stoop house in one afternoon, and though it's effective in protecting a lot of garden space, it remains a temporary structure. This greenhouse will take one person a weekend to lay out and establish beds. It will take two people another weekend to assemble and cover. And it will take one person a third casual weekend to put together the doors and vent covers. When the greenhouse is done and functioning, it may look a little like a stoop house, but it will differ vastly in performance.

The beauty of this basic structure is its flexibility. Though I set my garden greenhouse up with growing beds, some people set theirs up with tables or clear areas for growing seedlings in trays. Also, 20-foot-long (6 m) pieces of PVC pipe allow for a structure that's 14 feet (4.2 m) wide. But there's really no limitation on its length. I made my greenhouse 20 feet (6 m) long because that's the size that fits in the spot where I wanted it, but it can be made as long as you wish. You could make the width narrower, but you need to experiment with the shape of the arch when you bend the PVC pipe to make sure it's going to work the way you wish. Also, you can't make this greenhouse wider than 14 feet (4.2 m) by adding connectors and 10-foot sections (3 m) to make a longer PVC rib, because PVC ribs longer than 20 feet (6 m) are structurally weak. If you want a greenhouse wider than 14 feet (4.2 m), you need to look at commercially produced greenhouses that use metal ribs.

Choosing the Site and Layout

The first thing you need to do is determine how long you want this structure to be. Steve Painter made his 24 feet (7.2 m) long. I wanted my greenhouse to fit in a specific space and that took up 20 feet (6 m), so I knew my greenhouse would measure 14 x 20 feet (4.2 x 6 m).

I also knew that I wanted to establish three growing beds inside my greenhouse. As it happened, I had one garden bed already established in the spot where I wanted the greenhouse, so I incorporated it into the scheme. With 280 square feet (25 m²) to work with, I had considerable flexibility on the layout and width of the beds and paths. My final design incorporated a 4¹/₂-foot-wide (1.4 m) bed along the north side that's superinsulated to grow greens during the coldest part of the winter. I created two paths, each 16 inches (40.6 cm) wide, with a 3-foot-wide (.9 m) bed on the south side and an island bed in the middle about 3¹/₂ feet (1 m) wide. As you're considering the layout of your greenhouse, make note of its eventual alignment to the south. There has been a considerable amount of discussion over the years regarding this alignment. Many professional greenhouse operators build their greenhouses north to south, but there are others who build them east to west. There are equally good reasons for doing it both ways. But the bottom line (in my mind, at least) is this question you need to ask yourself: What will the alignment be that works best with my property? Regardless of how your greenhouse sits, you'll have a terrific enhanced growing environment if you have a solid eight hours of sun. My own greenhouse sits on a hillside that slopes down to the south-southwest. I ran the greenhouse parallel to the hill because that worked best to achieve level growing beds. Overall I have excellent light, which hits all three growing beds all day long. Even though it isn't set up exactly parallel or perpendicular to the north to south axis, I am very satisfied because it works well with my site.

Once you've decided your alignment, and perimeter, map out several different configurations for beds and paths based on what you want to grow and how you want to use the structure.

This is the site I chose for my greenhouse. The existing bed is to the left.

The Layout of Your Garden Greenhouse Footprint

Here's how to establish the perimeter on the alignment you choose (it's easier to do this with the assistance of a friend):

❧ Drive a rebar stake at one corner where you've decided to place the greenhouse.

❧ Drive another stake into the ground 20 feet (6 m) away (or however long you wish to make it) to create one edge.

❧ Drive stakes 14 feet (4.2 m) from each corner, and adjust them so they're 20 feet (6 m) from each other as well.

❧ Take diagonal measurements (see page 27) and adjust the stakes to the new perimeter. Then, drive the stakes 6 inches (15.2 cm) into the ground to make sure they stay there during the initial construction process.

Establishing the Layout of the Beds

❧ If the greenhouse will be on a site that has grass, don't worry about it; we'll take care of that later.

❧ Take a long rope and wrap it around the four stakes to see what the outline of the greenhouse will look like.

❧ Take another rope or a spool of twine and lay it on the ground in the configuration showing the outline of the beds. Some people like pathways on the outside of the beds along the curved side of the greenhouse. I chose not to do this because I didn't want to lose the growing space on two extra paths.

❧ Determine where your door or doors will be in the ends of the greenhouse, and leave plenty of pathways to get in and out of the structure. You can put doors at both ends of your greenhouse for simple venting. I wanted one door on the south end and a work area at the north end that included a bench to sit on when it wasn't holding seedling trays.

❧ With the ropes laid down showing bed placement, walk around in the greenhouse-to-be and see how it feels. Get down on your knees and reach over the edge of the beds to see if you have ample room to work.

Preparing Your Beds

Once the plastic is in place covering the PVC ribs, you can still work the beds, but it's much easier to get the beds established the way you want them before the structure is in the way. If you're in a hurry, you can remove the sod and proceed. You can rent a sod cutter at the local equipment rental outlet to easily shave the sod off to bare ground. When you remove the sod, you can either transplant it in new areas of your lawn that are bare, or send the sod to your compost bin. But an easier way to get it done, if you have four or five weeks to let the beds sit idly before continuing construction, is to do the following work and cover it all with cardboard to kill grass and suppress weeds. Regardless of whether you're removing sod or covering the ground with cardboard to smother the grass, here's how to prepare your growing beds:

𝕤 Determine the width and length of each bed. Spread one coffee can each of lime, rock phosphate, and greensand for each 100 square feet (9m²) of bed.

𝕤 Add 3 inches (7.6 cm) of compost or well-aged manure over each bed.

𝕤 If you're in a hurry, and you've already removed the sod, turn the soil over so the amendments, compost, and soil are all mixed together to a depth of about 8 inches (20.3 cm). Cover the whole affair now with cardboard to keep any weeds from sprouting in your new beds.

𝕤 If you've left sod in place, saturate the entire area inside the greenhouse perimeter with water from a sprinkler, and cover the area with cardboard to kill the grass and to keep weeds from sprouting from the compost. At this point you should have a rectangle patch of ground the size of the footprint of your future greenhouse, and the whole affair should be covered with big pieces of cardboard to suppress weeds in your beds.

Building Your Greenhouse

Before you talk yourself out of realizing your dream of a permanent greenhouse in your garden, I promise that this greenhouse is significantly easier to put together than you would imagine, and it's pretty cheap compared to the same-sized greenhouses that are on the market today.

The design details of my greenhouse came from an organic farmer named Steve Painter who lives in the mountains of North Carolina. He's been experimenting with this system of making greenhouses for many years and was one of the first folks in my region who saw the value of using PVC to build cost-effective greenhouse structures. The first greenhouse he built using this system went up in 1970. Though he has to change the plastic every three or four years (as everyone needs to do), the structure's still in excellent shape today.

Materials and Tools for a 14 x 20-foot (4.2 x 6 m) Garden Greenhouse

PIPES, REBAR, AND CONNECTORS

- 6 pieces 1¼-inch (3.2 cm) EMT pipe, 10 feet (3 m) long, for hoop connectors (you'll them cut in half to get 12 pieces)
- 6 pieces ¾-inch (1.9 cm) EMT pipe, 10 feet (3 m) long, for bracing the frame
- 3 EMT couplings, ¾ inch (1.9 cm) long
- 6 pieces 1½-inch (3.8 cm) PVC pipe, 20 feet (6 m) long, for frame★
- 2 pieces 1-inch (2.5 cm) PVC pipe lengths, each 6 inches (15.2 cm) longer than the length of the greenhouse (using connection junctions)
- Several dozen rebar stakes, 2 feet (.6 m) long, for bed construction
- 4 pieces ⅜-inch (1 cm) rebar, 20 feet (6 m) long, for crossbracing

★ This allows for ribs that are 4 feet (1.2 m) on center. A 24-foot-long (7.2 m) greenhouse would have seven ribs, and a 16-foot-long (4.8 m) greenhouse would have five ribs.

LUMBER

- 2 pieces 2 x 8 southern yellow pine (or other suitable lumber), 20 feet (6 m) long, for perimeter frame
- 2 pieces 2 x 8 southern yellow pine, 14 feet (4.2 m) long, for perimeter frame
- At least 90 linear feet (18 m) 2 x 6 southern yellow pine, for bed construction
- 2 pieces 2 x 4 framing lumber, 20 feet (6 m) long, for tops of side vents
- At least 8 pieces 1 x 4 pine, 8 feet (2.4 m) long, for door and vents
- 15 pieces 2 x 4 southern yellow pine, 10 feet (3 m) long, for framing end walls
- Several 1 x 2 strips of lumber, for attaching plastic to frame

ADDITIONAL MATERIALS

- String
- 12 "C" brackets, 1½ inches (3.8 cm)
- 1¼-inch (3.2 cm) roofing nails
- #20 galvanized ring shank nails
- Duct tape
- 2 sheets 2-inch-thick (5.1 cm) foil-backed or blue rigid insulation (optional)
- 12 carriage bolts with nuts and washers, 5/16 x 4 inches (8 mm x 10.2 cm)
- Roll of nylon cord or heavy wire
- Thermostatically controlled attic fan (optional)
- 2-foot-wide (.6 m) chicken wire, 50 feet (15 m) long, for covering vents
- Electrical hookup parts consisting of floodlight and outlet (consult with an electrician) (optional)

- 6-mil greenhouse plastic
- 6 luggage straps with quick closers, for side vents

TOOLS

- Saw
- Tape measure
- Safety glasses
- Hacksaw
- Sledgehammer
- Carpenter's level
- Hammer
- Drill
- Utility knife
- Stapler
- 2 stepladders

Installing the EMT Pipe

Your next step is to install the ground-to-hoop connections.

§ Cut the EMT pieces in half with the hacksaw. Make sure you use safety glasses to keep metal splinters out of your eyes. If you install a metal-cutting blade in a circular saw, you can make quicker work of this cutting process, but the metal pipes are thin enough for a hacksaw to do the job fairly easily.

§ Your next goal is to pound four pipes halfway into the ground at each corner of the greenhouse. Each pipe needs to be slightly angled toward the opposite side to create an arch when the end of each PVC pipe is slipped over the top of each. This business of determining the correct angle is not an exact science. If you're unsure of the angle, test the shape by bending a piece of PVC and sliding the

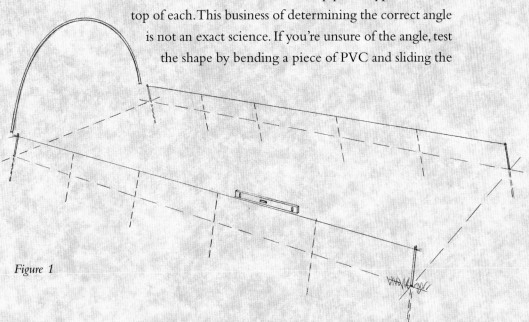

Figure 1

ends over the first pair of EMT pipes to see if you like the shape of the result-ing hoop. At this point you should have four pipes installed in the corners of the long sides of the outline of the greenhouse, slanted toward the pipes on the other side of the greenhouse 14 feet (4.2 m) away.

✥ Stretch and attach a piece of string from both the top and bottom of one EMT pipe to the EMT pipe that's on the same side (20 feet [6 m] away). Repeat on the other side. These are guidelines so the rest of the pipes will be at the same exact angles as the outside pipes.

✥ Using the level, get the top string level, adjusting the position of the line on the end pipes that you installed first.

✥ Take the rest of the pipes and lay them on the ground at 4-foot (1.2 m) inter-vals, so you know exactly where they'll be placed.

✥ Using the strings as a guide, pound each pipe into the ground until they are level with the top string. Have a friend hold a piece of scrap wood on top of the pipes to protect them from disfiguring. You should now have a pair of level, parallel lines of pipe, which are angled toward the middle.

You can hammer the EMT pipes into the ground yourself, though it's probably best to have a friend hold a piece of wood on top of the pipe you're hammering to keep the pipe from getting disfigured.

Framing the Beds and Preparing Them for Growing

You now want to set up the base of the structure and frame the beds.

🌱 Lay the 20-foot (6 m) 2 x 8s along the outside of the EMT pipes so the boards are sitting on the ground and leaning against the pipes. Place the carpenter's level on them and determine what's required to make them level. You'll probably need to excavate under the high side to drop them to a level position.

🌱 Once the boards are level, attach one "C" clamp around each EMT pipe. Then attach the clamp to the inside of the boards with the roofing nails. Cut the ends of the boards off flush with the outside of the end pipes.

🌱 Lay the 14-foot (4.2 m) 2 x 8s on the ends to connect the sides of the greenhouse together. Don't worry whether or not they're level, as long as these boards are sitting flat on the ground. Mark the ends where they go past the sideboards that are attached to the EMT pipe, and cut them on the lines. Put the end boards back in place and nail the corners with three galvanized nails at each junction.

🌱 Remove the cardboard so you can see the outline of where the beds will be located. Your next step will be to install boards that define the beds and separate them from the pathways. You could plant directly into the ground without setting up boards around the perimeter of the beds, but the wooden-framed beds will allow you to conveniently add organic matter without its spreading into the narrow pathways. Also, they create a frame from which tunnels can be attached later to create further enhanced growing environments inside your garden greenhouse. You can hold up the sides with rebar stakes.

Note rebar stakes holding the perimeter of the greenhouse and bed sides in place

Path Treatment

At this point, you should have your beds framed. You need to think about what you'll use to suppress grass on the pathways. You can continue using cardboard to suppress growth on the sides, but you'll find that it isn't terribly pleasing to the eye, and it'll need to be replaced periodically.

Many commercial greenhouses now have a black landscape fabric laid on the pathways, which does a great job of suppressing the growth of grass and weeds, and it allows water from your hose to pass through without creating a muddy mess. There are "U"-shaped staples that are often sold with this material, and they offer a great way to keep the fabric stretched and attached to the ground. If you plan to use this fabric only, you should consider doubling it to stand years of traffic.

Many folks cover the landscape fabric with 6 to 8 inches (15.2 to 20.3 cm) of pea-sized gravel. It looks good and drains water well. You might be persuaded to cover the pathways with bark mulch. I would advise against organic mulch of any type because it can encourage the growth of algae and fungus in the elevated level of humidity and heat found in greenhouses.

Installing the Hoops

The pieces of PVC pipe that make the hoop structure are unwieldy and require two people to install them. Take one end of the first pipe and slide it over the edge of one corner of EMT pipe. Pull the opposite end down and muscle it into position so it slides over the top of the EMT pipe on the opposite side. You'll find that the work you did in leveling the lumber edges pays off now because it ensures that the hoops are all in the same shape. You have the opportunity to raise and lower the height of the greenhouse by adjusting the distance that the PVC pipes stop above the top of the boards that are attached to the EMT pipes. As you adjust the height of the PVC pipes, make sure that you have at least 8 inches (20.3 cm) of EMT pipe inside the PVC pipe when you finally decide on the position of the hoops. It's a good idea to temporarily secure the PVC to the EMT with duct tape so it'll hold in the correct position. Make sure that the tops of all the PVC pipes are parallel.

Final Bed Preparation and Optional Insulation

The growing bed in the middle of the greenhouse will be easy to work any time. But this is your last chance to conveniently work your side-growing beds before it becomes difficult because of the plastic that'll be attached to the hoops. Now's also the time to remove any cardboard and prepare the soil for planting. If you have any more compost, you can add it to the beds and turn the soil over until they're prepared to your satisfaction. Once you've prepared the beds for planting, you can put them into a holding pattern until you want to plant them by covering the soil with cardboard or a straw mulch to suppress weeds and to keep the soil friable. If you do this, there won't be a crust that develops on the surface of soil that isn't planted immediately.

Insulation nailed to the sideboards

Now's also the time to consider bed insulation. My garden greenhouse has one insulated bed. The purpose is to have a superinsulated growing space for midwinter growing. I didn't see a need to insulate other beds that could be used in the less-severe parts of the winter. There's no question that insulating into the ground will keep the cold out, and the deeper you go, the more effective your insulation will be. You could cover the outsides of the beds with insulation, but I choose to line the inside of the beds to hide it.

I use a foil-backed, rigid insulation that's available at a reasonable price at my local home center. It comes in 4 x 8-foot (1.2 x 2.4 m) sheets, and it's 2 inches (5.1 cm) thick. I cut it to 16-inch (40.6 cm) widths to get three 8-foot (2.4 m) pieces out of each piece. (With my 20-foot-long [6 m] bed, I insulated it with two sheets.) You can also use a rigid insulation that's light blue, or a foil-faced material. What you don't want to use is a white insulation that looks like packing peanuts pressed together. This white insulation will come apart easily once it gets wet.

Wood strips are nailed through the insulation and attached to the outside frameboards. Wood caps are then installed, covering the boards and insulation. Finally, the ammended soil is added back into the bed.

As an organic gardener, I am always concerned about using materials that could add toxins to my soil. I checked pretty carefully and am satisfied that rigid insulation is stable when used in this manner, and it won't outgas or leach chemicals into the soil.

You'll still see the top of the insulation after the soil's replaced against it. I covered my rigid insulation by setting up 1 x 6-inch (2.5 x 15.2 cm) strips of rough pine against the sides of the insulation and then placing a 1 x 6-inch (2.5 x 15.2 cm) cap over the top. The resulting ledge looks good and gives me a comfortable spot to sit when working the bed or harvesting. And, of course, the soil stays significantly warmer than the soil in my other two beds.

Setting Up for Side Vents

Side vents allow the greenhouse to get plenty of cross-ventilation. They also allow the greenhouse to be used in the summer to grow warm-weather crops. It would be too hot to grow in it past spring if the side vents weren't there.

§ At each corner of the greenhouse, from the top of the wooden boards framing the greenhouse, measure up the sides of the hoop ribs and place a mark at 15 inches (38.1 cm). Tie a string to the rib at that point, and attach it to the hoop at the opposite end (see figure 2). Make sure that this line isn't above the top of the EMT pipe that's inside the PVC pipe. If it's above the top end of the EMT, move this line down so it is at least 8 inches (20.3 cm) from the top of the EMT.

§ Drill a ⅛-inch (3 mm) pilot hole through the middle of the PVC pipe where the string line crosses each hoop. You'll do this on both sides. As you go through the plastic PVC pipe, you'll notice that you're also going through the metal EMT. Be careful not to stress the pipe at this point because you might shatter the plastic PVC. You won't have problems if you go slowly and let the drill bit do the work. When the hole is drilled, follow it with a ⅜-inch (1 cm) drill bit to increase the size of the hole. Put a nail through the hole to keep the hole aligned, and move on to the next hoop to cut a hole. A word of caution: When drilling the second, larger hole through the two pipes, make sure you come in from both sides because the PVC pipe may crack if the larger drill bit is cutting from the inside. The photo on the left shows the resulting crack in the PVC and the remedy of drilling a hole at the top of the crack to keep the damage from spreading. The structural integrity of the PVC pipe is

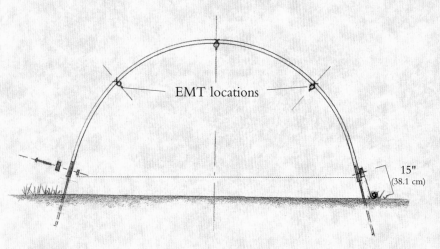

EMT locations

15"
(38.1 cm)

Figure 2

somewhat compromised with a repaired crack such as this, but it'll be okay if you use this damaged pipe toward the middle of the structure, where it will receive less stress.)

🖙 With an assistant, hold the 20-foot (6 m) 2 x 4 up so it's centered in the holes that you've just drilled. From the inside, drill through the new hole in the pipe so a hole emerges through the center of the 2 x 4. Remove the drill bit and insert a carriage bolt through from the outside and install the washer and nut on the inside to secure it.

🖙 You'll be installing a 2 x 4 on each side of the greenhouse. The photo above shows one side of the 2 x 4 in place. The purpose of this 2 x 4 is to add structural integrity to the frame and to have a place to attach the greenhouse plastic to it, while allowing the space under it to become a vent that can be opened up as warm weather arrives.

The side vent in this greenhouse is open to keep the Austrian winter peas from suffering from too much accumulated heat.

Adding Structural Integrity

🖙 Attach the 10-foot (3 m) pieces of $^3/_4$-inch (1.9 cm) EMT pipe together with junction connections so you have three 20-foot (6 m) pieces. These pipes will be attached to the hoops so the whole structure has a single attached framework.

🖙 Drill a $^3/_{16}$-inch (5 mm) hole through each 20-foot (6 m) piece, 1 inch (2.5 cm) from each end. Mark and drill holes every 4 feet (1.2 m) from the end of the pipe. With the help of a friend, hold one of the predrilled EMT sections up to the underside of the ribs in the center.

🖙 Run wire several times around the PVC rib and through the end holes of the EMT. Twist the ends of the wire together on the underside of the two intersect-

ing pipes, and trim the ends. Make a wired connection at each junction.

🎍 On the outside of the ribs, mark the halfway point between the top EMT rod you just installed and the top of the 2 x 4 that was bolted through the ribs earlier. Do this on both sides of the greenhouse. Hold the predrilled EMT rods against the inside of the ribs and wire the junction in the same way as you wired the top EMT rod (see figure 2 on page 98).

Framing the End Walls

You're now ready to install framing to the end walls. Your first task is to set up the framing so you can open up as much of these walls for venting as possible. Certainly the door can be opened in warm weather, but an open door is also an invitation to nearby animals, unless you have a screen door as well. A simpler alternative is to plan the door to be set up with a top panel that's hinged to allow you to vent through part of the door without opening up the greenhouse to unwanted pets. Your door should be placed so you can have a vent panel built in next to the door. Remember also that hot air rises, and the quickest way to get that hot air out of the greenhouse is by building vents at the peaks when you frame the ends.

Your door should be about 3 feet (.9 m) wide to allow easy access. You should also plan to make it as tall as you can to create more vent space. The vents on each side of the door should be set up so when you open a vent door, it can swing down without hitting the ground.

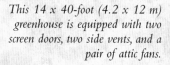

This 14 x 40-foot (4.2 x 12 m) greenhouse is equipped with two screen doors, two side vents, and a pair of attic fans.

Once you've clearly considered where you want vents, doors, and accoutrements to be located on the end walls, you can then do the framing. Here are the steps to get the end walls framed:

🖐 Determine the position of your door on the bottom board. Using the carpenter's level, mark the top point directly above on the hoop overhead. Measure over 36 inches (.9 m) to allow for a large enough door to comfortably move compost in and produce out. Mark those points at the top hoop and bottom boards. Cut, fit, and install two vertical pieces of 2 x 4 at these points. Nail them to the bottom boards.

🖐 Once the vertical pieces are in place, use 2 x 4s to complete the framing of the ends according to your design.

🖐 The point to remember here is that a perfect fit inside the hoop on the end wall framing isn't critical. What is critical is that all connections are solid. You can attach connections to the hoop where they touch by wiring.

Installing a Fan

If you're going to include a fan for venting, make sure you take that into account when framing the end walls. You can do without an electric fan, but a temperature-controlled fan helps maximize the greenhouse's ability to release hot air on those really sunny days. Fans manufactured for in-wall installation are very reasonably priced and they move a lot of air. Mine's a simple attic fan that moves 1,500 cubic feet (42.5 cubic meters) per minute and will get the hot air out very quickly. My temperature-controlled fan is my safety valve to get rid of hot air if I'm not there to open vents if there's a change in weather. You'll need to have an electrician wire your greenhouse for electricity first.

You could potentially use the automatic vent openers that I discussed in the cold frame chapter, but the cost to get enough to vent adequately would more than pay for the fan and wire needed to rig an electrical unit. And chances are pretty good that they still wouldn't move the hot air as quickly as you need to move it when temperatures escalate.

A Final Structural Detail

At this point, the end walls are up, and the EMT pipe is wired to the PVC hoops. The structure is reasonably sound, but it needs to be cross-braced to make it completely solid.

🖐 Take a 20-foot (6 m) piece of rebar and fit it into the pocket on the inside corner of the greenhouse where the first PVC hoop meets the end wall. Take the opposite end of the rebar, arch it, and move it to the center of the green-

Rebar, angling up from each corner and tied to every junction of PVC, EMT, and rebar, creates an even stronger structure.

house. The rebar should now be at a 45° angle to the sides and ends. Push the rebar up against the bottom of the hoops and attach it wherever it intersects with a hoop, EMT pipe, or other rebar, cross-bracing using wire to make it secure. Run a similar piece from each corner. This cross-bracing gives the final bit of structural integrity, and it'll provide a place from which to hang potted plants.

Animal-Proofing the Greenhouse

You may find that you'll want to linger in your garden greenhouse's enhanced environment on sunny days when it's too cold to be outside. Animals also enjoy hanging out in this space, but you won't want them to be there when you aren't around. So, after you've framed the end walls, but before you attach the plastic, animal-proof your greenhouse.

The long space on each side that's below the bolted 2 x 4s and above the outside border of the greenhouse will be a vent that can be opened on warm days. Cover this space with wire fencing to create a barrier for unwanted animals. I use chicken wire. It's reasonably priced, and the holes are small enough to keep all but the smallest critters out.

✺ Install the fencing on the inside of the hoops so it doesn't rub against the plastic covering. With the help of a friend, unroll the fencing halfway down the length of the greenhouse and hold it in position to get it set straight.

✺ Begin by stapling it to the top of the sideboard along the bottom of the bed and the 2 x 4 above it. Unroll the wire to the end of the greenhouse, and with the wire cutters, cut off enough to allow you to get to the opposite end wall. Pull it taut at the opposite end from which you started, and have the second person staple it at the top and bottom every 10 inches (25.4 cm). This is a temporary attachment. Do the other side the same way.

✺ Nail 1 x 2 strips cut to length between the ribs over the top and bottom sides of the fencing where it's stapled. Save the leftover fencing and 1 x 2 strips to cover vent openings on the end walls.

Electrical Vent and Light Hook Up

It's often dark by the time I get home from work in the winter. In order to be able to harvest veggies for dinner, I found a low-budget exterior floodlight to be a very useful addition to my greenhouse. If you want light, hire an electrician to hook up your thermostatically controlled attic fan as well. My electrician also set me up with a plug outlet that's appropriate for exterior use.

Covering the Framework

Once you have set up the sides and the beds to your liking, and everything's in order, it's finally time to cover the greenhouse. You'll need a reasonably warm day so the plastic isn't stiff and a time when there's no wind. You'll also need at least a couple of friends to help, though four people will make the job easy.

Over the years, I've helped friends cover or re-cover greenhouses at least 20 times. I've found that no matter how calm the conditions are, as soon as the plastic's unrolled and we're committed, the wind will start to blow. This is a cruel fact, and it's why you need to be completely prepared when you start before you ever open up the plastic covering.

§ Make sure you have wooden strips to attach at the 2 x 4s on the sides and #4 galvanized nails to secure them. Make sure you also have a staple gun that works and plenty of ³/₈-inch (1 cm) staples. Make sure you have a stepladder at each end of the greenhouse that's tall enough for you to easily see above the top. Make sure you have a plan and have discussed its procedure with the folks who have come to help you. You can also minimize the chances for wind if you get started by 9 a.m.

§ Cover the end walls first. Use the utility knife to cut two pieces to fit. Stretch the plastic along the bottom and over the top. Staple the bottom first and pull the plastic taut over the top edge. Roll the edges of the plastic to give more material for the staples to penetrate. Place staples at 6-inch (15.2 cm) intervals around the perimeter and around all door and vent openings. Staple only into the lumber, not the PVC pipe.

§ Spread the piece of plastic to go over the ribs on the side from which the breeze is coming. Have two people hold down the bottom while two other people pull the plastic over the top. Two people should climb the stepladders in the middle of the two ends to

help align the plastic. If there are fold lines on the plastic, you can use them to make sure the plastic is running parallel to the structure. When it's aligned to your satisfaction, with equal amounts hanging over the ends, pull the top tight at both end walls and set several staples at the top only. Put tension on all four corners simultaneously until you have a smooth, even tautness over the whole structure.

§ On the sides of the greenhouse you need to make sure that the bottom edge to be stapled will be on the 2 x 4, rather than the bottom of the board that's touching the ground. Roll the edge under where it meets the 2 x 4 and staple it. Staple securely along the 2 x 4 and pull the covering tight to attach to the 2 x 4 on the opposite side. Pull the ends tight over the end walls where you'll attach with staples as well. Trim enough plastic off the end walls to leave 6 inches (15.2 cm) hanging. Fold excess plastic over at the point where the end wall meets the first rib and staple carefully to secure unruly ends.

§ At this point, plastic should be covering the whole structure. It's stretched tightly over the doors and vents on the end walls, and it's stretched over the ribs down to the 2 x 4. You now need to make sure that the plastic stays in place. Nail 1 x 2 strips of wood wherever there's an overlap or a break in the plastic. Nail the strips over the plastic at 12-inch (30.5 cm) intervals across the 2 x 4 above the vent and along the bottom board on the end walls.

§ On the end walls, cut an "x" across the middle of the vent and door openings. Fold the four tabs into the openings and staple them to the sides of the openings. Attach 1 x 2 strips on the inside of the openings and nail them to secure the plastic. Trim off the excess plastic.

Setting Up Vent Flap Rollers

At this point, the entire greenhouse should be covered in plastic up to the 2 x 4s that run along the sides. You'll now set up flaps that can be rolled up the sides of the greenhouse from the ground to the bottom of the horizontal 2 x 4 to create a vent that can be opened on warm days and closed on cold days.

§ Connect sections of PVC pipe with connector junctions until the total length is 6 inches (15.2 cm) longer than the total length of the greenhouse. In my case, this added up to 20½ feet (6 m, 15.2 cm) and it required that I glue a 6-inch (15.2 cm) piece of PVC in the middle of two 10-foot (3 m) sections, connected with two connector junctions. Make up one for each side.

§ Prepare two strips of 1 x 2 that are the length of the greenhouse.

§ Cut two pieces of greenhouse plastic the length of the PVC pipe and 1 foot (30.5 cm) wider than the side vent.

§ On a flat surface, roll the plastic around the length of 1 x 2, and staple the plastic to the wood. Along the opposite edge, tape the PVC pipe to the outer edge of the plastic (figure 3). With the help of a friend, place the plastic-wrapped section of 1 x 2 against the 2 x 4 and attach it securely with nails every 10 inches (25.4 cm). The PVC-covered end of the plastic will hang down to the ground, creating a vent cover over the long horizontal vent (figure 4).

§ Set up three straps with quick closers on each vent. Attach over and under the side vent flaps with both ends attached to the 2 x 4 above the side vents. These should be placed in the middle and 2 feet (.6 m) in from each end. The purpose of these is to allow you to secure the side flaps at any height in a short amount of time. It'll collect water unless it's rolled under as it's raised.

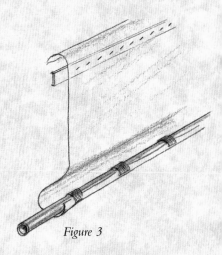

Figure 3

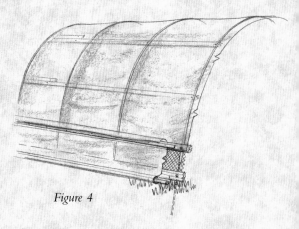

Figure 4

Manufacturing and Installing Door and Vent Covers

At this point, you should have a fully covered greenhouse. It's now time to build the door and vent doors. Begin by reading the section on assembling panels (page 70). Using the methods described there, you should measure the openings you wish to cover and add 3 inches (7.6 cm) to the width and height measurement. This extra size will allow you to overlap your panel in the closed position to keep cracks to a minimum. If you have an opening larger than 3 x 3 feet (.9 x .9 m), you should install a divider to give the panel structural integrity. Once the panels are assembled, you can simply wrap them up in scraps

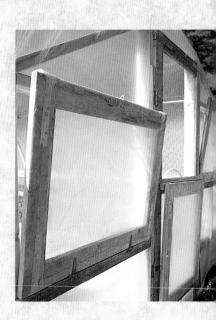

of greenhouse plastic and staple to secure them. Attach galvanized hinges and hooks to keep them open and closed, and you're in business.

Greenhouse Considerations

§ One of the fundamentals of season extension is that every layer of material over a growing area moves the plants to a climate 1½ gardening zones to the south. Once you've enclosed your greenhouse, you're in a wind-free environment that allows additional layers to be placed over growing areas without having to worry about wind. This makes a much simpler application of additional layers because you don't need to be staking or schlepping a large number of rocks or bricks. But it also means that you need to be careful not to set up an environment that's too stifling when the sun comes out after a bitterly cold night.

An extra layer of plastic is supported by ¹/₂-inch (1.3 cm) PVC pipe ribs. Note the end wall with vent openings and opened vent panel in the door.

§ I have used wire hoops and floaters to add second layers inside my greenhouse, and they have their value. I have also laid floaters directly over plants in the greenhouse, as many other hardy gardeners do, and have been very satisfied with the results. For one thing, temperatures generated under floaters are more moderate than under a second layer of plastic, which means your plants aren't going to be as susceptible to the wilting effect of high temperatures.

§ For many years, I've used a high/low thermometer that has to be reset each day. I've kept it on the north side of my house where it isn't affected by the sun. It has given me a good sense of what my plants can endure as temperatures drop. In the last few years, digital high/low thermometers have come on the market, and they're very reasonable. They can be found at the local home or garden center, and you shouldn't be without one. Mine is mounted out of the direct sunlight on the backside of the south wall of the greenhouse with a remote wire out leading to the north side. With these wonderful digital gizmos, you can now get inside and outside, and maximum and minimum temperatures any time you wish.

§ Celebrated market gardener Eliot Coleman grows crops during the coldest parts of the year inside three large, single-layered, unheated greenhouses. All three structures are on tracks that allow Coleman to drag the structures with a tractor over three positions of raised beds. It's an elegant remedy to the biggest flaw in using a greenhouse: the buildup of salinity in soil that is covered year after year by a greenhouse left in the same place. Salt and mineral buildup in your soil results in decreased soil quality (regardless of how much organic matter is added).

Most home gardeners like me don't have the room, resources, or inclination to set up a structure that can be moved, but the problem of salinity doesn't go away. One way you can give your soil a thorough flushing is to remove the cover for a summer. Because most greenhouse plastics last three or four years, changing coverings is a good opportunity to flush as well. Remove your plastic in late spring as the last frost of the winter is fast approaching. Make repeated plantings of cover crops of buckwheat throughout the summer, or a couple plantings of vetch or winter pea to give your soil some organic matter. Rains will help flush the buildup of salts in the soil, and you'll have renewed beds when you put on a new greenhouse skin in the fall.

Simply bend PVC hoops over a bed in your greenhouse and cover with plastic to add an additional layer to protect your cold-hardy greens at night or during extremely cold days. Note the chicken wire on the closed side vent—it helps keep out the critters when the vent's open.

Looking Through a Wider-Angle Lens: Other Strategies for Extending the Garden Season

MODIFYING CLIMATES IN CONTRAPTIONS isn't the only way to extend the gardening season. Over the years, I've happened upon strategies by observation, experimentation, and pure serendipity that allowed me to stretch the gardening season and enhance growing environments to significantly improve yields.

When You're in a Bind

Four or five years ago, during a glorious day in late winter when it felt like spring might actually be coming soon, I was tempted into buying two six-packs of broccoli seedlings. Any other time, I would've waited at least several more weeks to purchase seedlings for transplanting, but it felt so springlike I just couldn't help myself.

Three days later, winter returned with a vengeance. I had very little time to save my recently planted broccoli plants from freezing. Other parts of my garden were covered and safe, but I didn't have any contraption or fabric readily available to save the broccoli. Searching desperately for something to cover the baby broccoli plants, I saw the Christmas tree I hadn't gotten around to chopping up yet, and went to find my largest pruning shears. As snow began to fall, I spread the tree's branches loosely over the bed where I planted the broccoli. I had enough branches to cover all but three plants, which I figured were going to be a loss.

As it turned out, those plants went through another three weeks of snow, freezing rain, and consistently low temperatures. Remarkably enough, the three unprotected plants remained alive to go on to produce broccoli. But by the time warm weather really returned, the plants that were covered with the tree branches were twice as big and healthier than the unprotected broccoli. They went on to produce a crop several weeks earlier than the unprotected plants.

There are several things I gained from this experience. The first was another confirmation that cold-hardy crops are pretty darn rugged and can survive more extreme temperatures and weather than I would have imagined. I also had on-site confirmation that plants benefit from the protection of an enhanced growing environment. And finally, I realized that, in a pinch, one could generally find something close at hand to protect plants from cold weather.

Early fall is another time when you might be scrambling to find something to cover plants, such as basil, peppers, or tomatoes. Quite often they'll enjoy several more weeks of growth in balmy autumn weather if you can only get them through the trauma of one or two chilly nights when temperatures have dropped below freezing.

I know from personal experience that simply placing heavy blankets from the linen closet over your warm-weather plants will get them through the night and allow them to continue producing when moderate temperatures return. But don't use blankets from the linen closet. My own dear, persevering bride, Eleanor, appreciates the addition of fresh crops on the table after the arrival of first frosts, but she fails to fathom the necessity of using blankets from her linen closet to protect them!

In fact, there are plenty of materials that can be used when you're in a bind: cardboard boxes, tarps, a corral of hay bales, sheets of clear plastic, leaves, drop cloths, and even clusters of long stems of weeds. None of these will generate more heat, but they'll effectively keep existing heat from dissipating into the atmosphere. They'll also take the edge off wind damage, which is often more destructive to plants than the cold.

Straw-covered stick canopy
protecting kale after a snowfall

It's worth pointing out that a person's garden is different each year, as is the weather. Some years, the conditions are right, and a specific crop produces like mad and will keep producing in the warm days after the first frost, if it's been protected. This year we had a cold snap in late September that killed warm-weather plants that weren't covered. But then we had almost a full month before the next frost. Anyone who protected his or her plants during that first frost had another month of harvest. When you look at your garden, you'll not only realize that plant vigor is linked to how much stress it's allowed to undergo, but that most plants will recover from environmental stress (such as summer drought or winter bitter cold spells) much more quickly if they've been covered with something—even something unconventional.

Microclimates

Another way to look at your garden is to identify existing microclimates on your property and think about ways to establish new microclimates for the benefit of creating enhanced growing environments.

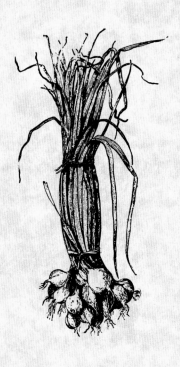

There was a time when our family hound's main criterion for finding a spot for his afternoon nap was the aesthetic value of our flowerbeds. It could be guaranteed that by 1:30 p.m. on any given day, he could be found sleeping in the middle of whatever perennials or annuals were at their peak of perfection. It's a wonder the dog survived Eleanor's wrath to live to a ripe old age. But as he grew older, I noticed that the beast developed a more discriminating criterion for finding a spot for his afternoon naps. Somewhere in his seventh or eighth winter, I noticed that Dakota had identified several places in the yard where conditions were right to increase the suitability for a warm spot to sleep. In doing so, he made me aware of some fundamental aspects of identifying microclimates.

It doesn't take a brain surgeon, or a dog named Dakota, to figure out areas that are the warmest spots on your property. Simple observation of places that melt first after a snowstorm will give you a pretty good idea of your local warm spots. Observing pets and other animals will further fine-tune your knowledge of your garden's microclimates.

Also think about places you've noticed where people have consciously changed or taken advantage of microclimates. Here are two popular examples:

The ancient Anasazi apartment complex of Mesa Verde in Colorado was built below an enormous, south-facing cliff. The builders of this aerie wonder created an enhanced living environment with the effective use of a site that already hosted a warmer microclimate, because of its sunny and protected location.

Arborvitae and privet hedge grown on the north side of an early 20th-century market garden

꽃 Old-time, classic family farms from the Midwestern United States will often have several acres of woods planted on the north side of the house and barns. These woods were planted to divert and diffuse winter winds that howled across the prairie. The woods created an enhanced growing environment for the people living there by designing a microclimate that changed the weather conditions of the farmyard organized on the south side of the woods.

Solid fences have bordered gardens for thousands of years. Though they kept out unwanted animals, they were most likely built to create new microclimates for the plants inside. Jeff Campbell from Scappoose, Oregon, surrounds his garden with an edible hedge of filbert nuts. The hedge creates an enhanced growing environment for his entire garden, and it produces a crop of nuts for his annual marathon of holiday fudge making. Planting shrubs or building fences at least on the north side of your garden can increase the effectiveness of your cold-hardy garden.

Timing

There's another aspect of this wider lens issue, and that's understanding the concept of timing. I have a friend in Rhode Island who has an apricot tree that bears fruit three out of every four years, even though these kinds of fruit trees don't normally fruit that far north. My friend accomplished this by planting the tree on the north side of a barn (the cold side), where it takes three to four weeks longer for the tree to flower than if it were on the south side, where it's warmer. The tree flowers when there's significantly less chance for a freeze to occur, which would render the tree fruitless for the year.

The Perpetual Salad Bed

Though my family loves lettuce, I gave up on saving seeds when I accidentally discovered a lazy man's strategy for growing lettuce. It happened one summer when I allowed a lettuce head to go to seed for saving and then forgot about it. By the time it was ready to be harvested for the seeds, the birds had attacked the seed head. What they didn't eat was scattered everywhere. I forgot about the lettuce seeds until a short time later when my garden bed erupted in a sea of lettuce seedlings. As fall progressed, more lettuce seedlings came up at their convenience. I transplanted the seedlings into garden beds, and we ate a bonanza of lettuce all fall. The following spring, even more lettuce seedlings came up. I continued to transplant these volunteers into open areas in the garden. Although all these seedlings came from the same plant, they came up at various times. That experience got me thinking about a way to have a perennial (and I use that term loosely) lettuce patch. In a nutshell, here's what I've come up with:

A perpetual salad bed in action

§ Go to your local garden shop and get three six-packs of open-pollinated lettuce, all different varieties. Make sure you choose open-pollinated varieties. Hybrids will not reproduce true to parent. Plant all 18 plants in an 20- to 30-square-foot (1.8 to 2.7 m²) portion of a bed that you've amended with compost. Keep the varieties separated for your own convenience (you don't need to worry about cross-pollination).

§ Harvest three of each variety and enjoy them with dinner. Pay close attention to the other nine plants, and mark the plant in each variety that's the last to go to seed. Destroy the six plants that were the quickest to go to seed. You'll know these plants are going to seed when a magnificent seed head begins to appear above the leaves. By saving the last plant of each variety that goes to seed, you've just selected the next generation of lettuce plants to be slower to bolt than the average lettuce plant. This means that you'll be able to harvest future generations longer into the warm weather

Cold (Really Cold) Weather Gardening

THE FIRST AGRICULTURAL experiments in the Arctic took place north of Hudson Bay in 1823. Explorer William Parry made use of a glass-sashed cold frame to grow cress, mustard, and peas during the two months of summer. Explorer Middleton Smith described using a cold frame during the summer of 1881 at Point Barrow, Alaska.

before they become bitter from bolting. (Don't let bolted lettuce continue growing in the garden unless you're allowing it to go to seed for the purpose of future lettuce generations.) Allow the three slow-to-bolt plants to go to seed. When the seeds are ripe, birds will feed on the seed heads, scattering seeds all over the garden area you've set aside for this purpose.

❧ Keep this garden area weed-free. You'll soon begin seeing tiny lettuce seedlings emerging. If the weather's hot (and the varieties you have used are adapted for cooler weather) you can count on most of these seedlings going bitter before you're able to enjoy them, unless you transplant them to cooler areas in the shade of tall plants. As the summer turns cooler, seedlings will emerge continually. You should ruthlessly thin seedlings as they come up so they're 2 inches (5.1 cm) apart, to allow ease in transplanting to other parts of the garden. The area you've set aside for this purpose is primarily a propagation plot.

❧ By fall, you should have a steady supply of lettuce seedlings that are coming up on their own. As the heat of summer passes, transplant newly emerging seedlings into beds that can be covered with floaters and tunnels, or into your cold frame for cold-weather harvest. Many of the seeds will lie dormant in your propagation plot throughout the winter and will sprout the following spring. At this point, it's important to save one plant from each variety to allow it to go to seed to perpetuate the system. During the second spring, you should attempt to plant three additional varieties of open-pollinated lettuces to add even further variety to your salads.

☙ Use compost that has heated up enough to kill weed seeds. Or add commercial compost that's more likely to be weedfree. Your goal is to reduce the competition for your seedlings. Also, once this system is established, you won't be turning the soil over, so get the soil the way you want it before you start.

☙ Even though you'll be planting lettuce varieties that have different days of maturity, you'll eventually see individual plants of all varieties maturing at their own rate. Some seeds will sprout immediately, and some will wait for months, or even years, to germinate. This perpetual salad system takes some effort to get established, but the rewards of significant numbers of volunteer seedlings for months, and even years, to come is well worth the effort.

Further Thoughts on Overwintering

There are two ways to use the strategy known as overwintering. One is the process of planting a crop in the fall early enough to get established, but late enough so it won't have the opportunity grow too much. The crop then goes into dormancy (as my first crop of overwintered spinach I discussed in the Getting Started chapter did), until spring weather returns. The other strategy protects biannual leafy plants, already growing in the garden, and keeps them alive through the winter to get a fresh flush of greens in the spring before they go to seed.

The process of overwintering late-fall planted greens is nothing new. The 1873 Shaker Seed Catalog carried three varieties of lettuces specifically suited for overwintering. By the time fall is well under way and frosts are occurring frequently, broadcast spinach, lettuce, arugula, and turnip greens in areas of the garden that have been left open for them. I find it easier to broadcast seeds and then cover them with $1/4$ inch (6 mm) of soil-less seed starting medium to give the seeds a weed-free environment to sprout through. Cover the areas with pieces of floater to increase and hasten germination, and then leave them alone. Within three weeks, the seedlings should be up but slowing considerably because of the cold. It is at this point that you should cover the floater-covered seeded areas loosely with hay or straw to give them protection for the next few frigid months. In late winter, when the sun is higher in the sky, and warm weather spells become more frequent, remove the straw protection from the floating row covers to allow the ground around the seedlings to warm up. Loosen up the floater covering so the plants have room to push the fabric up as they grow.

Overwintering is a simple and effective strategy that works in cooperation with the weather. In addition, it bypasses one extra seed-starting mess that takes up time in an already busy schedule.

OVERWINTERING GARLIC

My family considers garlic the fifth element of the universe. There's air, fire, water, earth, and garlic. Some might say that chocolate or coffee is the sixth element, but I believe the jury is still out on those.

August is the time to plant garlic because fall-planted garlic will produce bigger bulbs than spring-planted garlic (even though they harvest at the same time of midsummer). When looking for seed stock, you can use bulbs from your local grocery store to produce a wonderful crop of garlic. Some large grocery stores will carry garlic that's been sprayed to keep it from sprouting, and there's no way to tell which bulbs have been sprayed. You can be sure of getting good garlic for planting at your local farmer's market. Regardless of where you get it, look for solid large bulbs that are stored in open bins. Garlic needs to breathe, and it should not be used for seed if it has been wrapped in an airtight container.

For our family of four, I bring home about twenty bulbs to open up for seed stock. The kids and I break the bulbs apart and sort them into three piles:

Pile #1: Big cloves make big bulbs. Save the biggest cloves for seed, and don't waste the real estate on inferior-sized bulbs.

Pile #2: Medium-sized bulbs should go into a loosely capped jar in your kitchen cabinet to be used for cooking.

Pile #3: Let's face it. For those folks who are as busy as I am, it's a frustration to open those tiny cloves for cooking. We save those skinny cloves and plant them in little patches throughout the garden. When they sprout, we use scissors to cut off the green tops flush with the ground. These are as tasty as chives.

Plant cloves 6 inches (15.2 cm) apart and mulch with 6 inches (15.2 cm) of straw. Your garlic will start growing with the first showers, and they may send green shoots up before winter sets in. This crop will grow until the bitter cold causes it to go dormant. But the following spring will see it growing again until midsummer, when the tops begin to yellow, which is when you harvest it.

OVERWINTERING POTATOES

If you've ever grown potatoes in your garden, you've probably also overwintered potatoes by mistake. 'Taters that are overlooked during harvest will come up as volunteers the following year much earlier than spring-planted spuds.

The time to plant potatoes for overwintering is early fall. Seed potatoes aren't usually available this time of year at garden shops, but you can pick your favorite type of tuber at the grocery store for planting. Potatoes set out for over-wintering should be whole and the size of a large egg. Cut pieces of potato (a common method for getting several potato plants from large potatoes) are liable to rot in the cold, wet ground of winter. Set the seed potatoes, cover with fertile soil, and lay on a protective mulch of straw. Next year, treat the growing potatoes the way you treat spring-planted spuds, by filling the trench with soil around the necks of the plants as they grow.

Overwintering Biannuals

The second strategy I use for overwintering allows me to salvage kale, collards, and parsley that might otherwise expire if we experience a tough winter. Kale and parsley planted in the spring will produce leaves right through the fall because they thrive in cool temperatures. By early next spring, if kept vigorous by protection, they'll quickly grow a fresh crop of full-sized leaves on their mature rootstock. After that initial spring flush, these plants will go to seed because they're biannuals and destined to go to seed the second year. Kale (as well as collards and all varieties of cabbage) will form small, loose flowerets resembling broccoli a few days before turning into tiny yellow flowers. Those flowerets are tender, tasty, and wonderful in salads or lightly stir-fried. After flowering, they'll be good only for saving seeds.

To save these plants through the winter, cut back all growth late in the fall, allowing only 3 inches (7.6 cm) of the stems to show above the ground. Side-dress the stems with compost and surround them with straw to protect the plants until the ground begins to warm the following spring.

A Stone-Mulching Believer

The purpose of straw, wood chips, and grass mulch is to conserve water, suppress weeds, and keep the ground at moderate temperatures around plants so they are not stressed. Those mulches are used throughout the summer garden, but you don't want to use them in the winter because they insulate the ground and keep it from warming. In the winter, if you have a choice between those mulches, and no mulch, you should choose no mulch so the bare, dark ground can absorb as much heat as possible. Black plastic, IRT, and stone do the same things, but they also absorb and retain heat.

A number of years ago, I read an interesting article on stone mulching. It inspired me to try it in my garden. That following spring, I planted four water-

melon plants in one bed approximately 5 feet (1.5 m) apart. Around two plants I placed mulch hay, and around the other two I placed a solid circle of plate-sized stones radiating 2 feet (60 cm) from the plants. I watched the growth of all the plants carefully and couldn't see much difference between them. Looking under the mulch, I couldn't see much difference either—both stone and straw mulch resulted in soil that was weedless, loose, moist, and filled with happy earthworms. By the end of the summer though, I had achieved twice the production of watermelons with the stone mulch. That made a stone mulching believer out of me.

I use stone to mulch peppers, eggplants, squash, basil, and melons. I choose flat stones and install them at the time of planting. I look for flat pieces approx-

imately 2 inches (5.1 cm) thick. The fact of the matter is, the stones can be any shapes you wish. I prefer flat stones because they stack neatly in cairns when I'm not using them, and they look good on the beds when they're in use.

So how much does rock mulch change temperatures? Here's a comparison of various mulches and their impact on the soil. Temperatures were taken using bare soil as a control.

Large flat stones	1° warmer
Black plastic	1° warmer
IRT★	9° warmer
Clear plastic	at least 12° warmer
Straw	7° cooler

★ IRT is a fairly recent product. It's a red or black plastic-like material that allows water to penetrate, but keeps the sun out.

Thoughts on Temperature and Mulch

✺ Large, flat stones absorb heat and increase soil temperatures as well as black plastic, but because of the effects of UV radiation, black plastic is good for only one season. Stones can be used year after year and won't contribute to excess landfill waste.

✺ In Rhode Island, I made use of scrap pieces of a dark patio paving material called "bluestone" that I picked up from a landscaper pal. I noticed a significant difference in the heat from that material compared to the lighter-colored flat stones I was also using. This has made me wonder about the idea of painting some of my stones black to absorb more heat.

✺ Clear plastic is too intense for season extension when used as mulch. It creates a hot enough environment to kill seeds in soil.

✺ A stone-mulched area in the garden looks like a cobbled path until the plants fill in, so make sure visitors know they aren't supposed to step on it.

Seaweed Studies

Dr. T.L. Senn, professor emeritus of the Department of Horticulture at Clemson University, has studied the effect of foliar spraying of seaweed concentrate on various crops for many years. Although seaweed doesn't contain a large concentration of nitrogen, phosphorus, or potassium found in normal fertilizers, it does contain a wide variety of nutrients (such as iron, copper, zinc, molybdenum, boron, manganese, and cobalt) that are critical to plant development. Seaweed also contains a chelating compound known as *mannitol*, which has the ability to make critical micronutrients available in a form that plants can use immediately.

Foliar spraying appears to be most beneficial just before or just as plants encounter stress conditions such as flowering, fruiting, and (of special interest to cold-hardy gardeners) cold weather. Senn found that tomato plants that have been sprayed with diluted seaweed concentrate could survive temperatures as low as 29°F (-2°C) degrees, while their unsprayed brethren were wiped out by frost. One study showed plants surviving two such frosts, three nights in a row. A couple of degrees below freezing may not sound like a huge advantage, but the fact is that early frosts in the fall don't often drop more than that. And a foliar spraying of liquid seaweed concentrate, several times a week for three weeks before your anticipated first frost, gives you an edge if you've scrambled to make sure your warm-weather plants have the additional protection of a fabric or contraption already in place.

Squash in the Compost

I grew my first crops of butternut squash in the garden. I grew an acceptable amount of this tasty winter squash, and I felt the return was worth the growing space I lost from rambling vines in nearby beds. I attempted to trellis the vines the second year to save space, but I wasn't crazy about the time I had to spend tying up the squash and hanging truant vines. One spring, I noticed squash seedlings emerging from one of my compost piles. We were still expe-

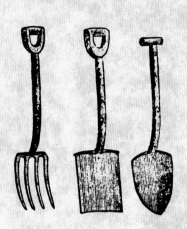

Pallet-able Compost Bins

I CREATE MY COMPOST BINS out of wooden pallets. I once heard that approximately the same amount of wood goes into making pallets as building homes, and whether or not that's true, I know they're easy to find. As you drive around business districts, peer along the sides and backs of businesses, and you'll soon start seeing piles of pallets waiting to be used or thrown in the landfill. If you ask at the business, they'll often allow you to take what you want for free, or they'll generally know where you can get them. Don't grab just any pallet. There's a tremendous variety of sizes and styles, so make sure you get three or four pallets that are the same. Simply wire the pallets together to create a cube that's about 4 square feet (.36 m²), and you have a perfect compost bin.

riencing late frosts, but the volunteer squash survived because of the heat generated by the compost. Beginning that spring, I stopped wasting real estate in the garden and started taking advantage of unused space by planting squash directly into my compost bins.

I usually have several compost bins that are in various stages of completion, and though it takes about twice as long to get a load of compost, I don't hasten the process by turning my piles. (It's not that I don't want compost in a hurry; I'm simply too lazy to turn it, and I'd rather use the time obtaining more organic matter to add to the bins.) When spring comes to my garden, there's always at least one bin that's hot from the composting action. There's generally a more mature bin that's still warm from the composting action that has recently taken place. The hot bin is the one in which I prefer to plant my winter squash. I'm able to plant this tender crop at least three weeks before the last expected spring frost because of the heat generated by the compost. Such an early planting produces at least one-third more crops.

Here's how to prepare an enhanced growing environment to get an early start for your winter squash:

🍂 Begin by spreading and slightly packing the organic matter inside the bin to make a flat planting area. Water the top of the compost thoroughly.

🍂 Make two depressions in the top of the organic matter about the size of serving bowls. Place about 1 gallon (3.8 L) of good, rich garden soil in each shallow depression, and shape it into a flat-topped mound. This soil will warm up, but it'll also act as an insulator for the seeds that could be harmed by the high heat being generated by microbial action below in the heart of the compost bin.

🌶 Plant three winter squash seeds into each mound, and water. Be careful not to wash the shape of the flat mound away. Place a piece of floater over the top of the planted compost pile, and hold the corners down with stones or bricks.

🌶 When the seedlings emerge, leave the two healthiest plants in each mound. You'll need to water more often because the bins dry out faster than garden beds. When the plants mature and are running wild over the sides of your bins, they'll show you if you've been negligent in watering by wilting their normally magnificent compost-fed leaves.

There are several benefits to using this system for growing winter squash. First of all, the squash love the fact that their roots are going down into pure squash food. Because of this, the plants I have grown in compost bins are always very healthy and generally quite resistant to insects that would prefer to attack less healthy plants. With an unlimited amount of food at their feet, my squash plants have always provided me with a bumper crop. Also, since the plants require water throughout the season, the compost in the bin gets more water, which works out to produce compost more quickly. Plus, the squash roots in the bins seem to produce compost that has a finer finish to it. And finally, you'll bask in the sunshine of your gardening pals' envy when they gawk and squawk at the magnificent sight of your lovely vine and squash blossom-covered compost bins.

An Effective Seed-Starting Mantra

If you're committed to the four-season garden challenge, chances are pretty good that you'll soon figure out that you need to start growing your own transplants. Garden centers sell plants for warm-weather gardeners. And by the time transplants comes to your local garden center, contraptions should already be filled with thriving plants. When the end of summer arrives, and you're planning on a fall garden, you won't find newly arrived seedlings at the garden center, because it's the end of the growing season for most folks. The bottom line here is that you need to be able to effectively produce seedling stock yourself if you want to get a dependable source of material to transplant to the garden out of season.

The first step to becoming independent of other sources for seedlings is to get a seed-starting system together that works. Here are some hints:

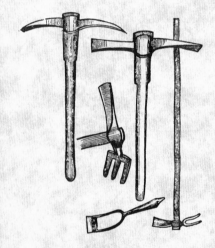

❧ If you've started plants in the past using various assortments of milk cartons, yogurt containers, etc., that sit precariously on south-facing windowsills, rethink your system and keep only what you use all the time.

❧ Run your seed-starting paraphernalia through the dishwasher before starting a new crop, to get rid of any fungal diseases that might be lurking.

❧ Keep a 45-gallon (171 L) plastic trash can filled with soil-less seed starting medium so you'll always be able to fill seed trays when the mood or need strikes.

❧ Use low-cost shop lights with common fluorescent fixtures (which are just as effective as the expensive "grow light" fixtures) to start seedlings.

❧ Use a cold frame to effectively grow seedlings in seed trays.

It doesn't matter how many contraptions you have for extending the season if you don't have seedlings to fill them when the time is ripe. My biggest challenge in getting into the seed-starting frame of mind that's necessary for effective season extension was to learn to start seedlings at the appropriate time in the spring and midsummer. After missing the mark enough times, I came up with a mantra that I sat down and repeated about a hundred times. That mantra is now indelibly imprinted on my brain, and it surfaces at the appropriate time to remind me of the need to begin seed-starting activities that'll give me the seedlings I need when they're required down the road. The mantra is this: "March and July until I die." What this means is that in March and July of each year, I will start my seedlings. Skeptical though you may be, this imprinted mantra has made me a more consistent seed starter. March may be too early in colder zones, and it may be too late in warmer zones. The same may hold true for July. The point is, create a mantra that works for you.

VEGETABLES FOR COLD WEATHER GARDENS

EARLY ON, IT BECAME CLEAR that although I could begin my tomato, basil, and squash season early under a contraption and/or extend the plants' harvest season with a devise of some sort that would protect them from an early frost, it would not be feasible to grow these heat-loving crops in the winter. Growing tomatoes and other warm-weather veggies through the winter requires a greenhouse that never goes below 45°F (7°C). And while tomatoes are raised commercially in this manner, I've never worked a structure where I could grow warm-weather crops through the dark of winter, and I don't know any home gardeners who do. Simply speaking, the commitment and cost are prohibitive and just not worth the effort for a home gardener. However, a little investigation shows that there are many vegetables that actually prefer growing in cool weather, and with a little help, they could handle the bitter cold of winter.

When conceiving this chapter, I considered addressing every veggie that's cold hardy and giving cultivation tips for each, like some sort of encyclopedia. But that format doesn't achieve my goal, which is for you to use this book as a

A bed of lettuce, claytonia, and spinach

springboard for a broader base of understanding of extending the gardening season. So instead, I'm going to tell you the easy way I learned about many of the veggies suitable for cultivation in the colder months of the year. I'll also talk briefly about the various hardy veggies, and I'll share with you my own veggie experiences as a home gardener with a busy schedule who eats out of the garden year-round.

The Roots of Vegetable Bigotry: A Case for Cold-Hardy Veggies

I believe my long-held aversion to kale was a simple case of vegetable bigotry that has its basis in childhood trauma. There are few among us who don't hold in their minds the image of themselves sitting alone at the dinner table, long since vacated by other family members. On the plate in front of you sits a mass of cold vegetables—carrots steamed to a mushy balsa-wood texture, a hardened pancake of yellow-green kale in cheese sauce, or perhaps collard greens cooked unmercifully and stuck to the plate with congealed bacon fat. You know you can't leave the table until the vegetable in question is consumed, and you face the very real possibility of spending the best years of puberty sitting at that lonely kitchen table watching as the world continues to turn without you.

If you think about it, most vegetable bigotry is associated with cold-hardy vegetables, and the largest complaint seems to be a perceived belief that such veggies are bitter or wood-textured. This bias persists, not because these veggies are inherently tough or bitter, but because they've been systematically harvested at the wrong time. This has gone on for so long that the public now assumes they're supposed to be bitter.

There's no question that collards, mustard greens, Brussels sprouts, cabbage, and kale will mature very well in the summer, but that doesn't mean they should be harvested in hot weather. The wonderful thing about these crops is that though they're bitter when harvested in the summer (to varying degrees), they'll be considerably sweeter after being hit by a couple of frosts in the fall. The reason for this is that the rate of respiration in hardy vegetables slows down in cool weather. Sugar (generated by photosynthesis) is the fuel that allows a plant to breathe. In times of high stress, hardy plants are using every bit of sugar available to stay alive. Bitterness is a result of sugar depletion during these periods of high stress when temperatures soar and the soil is dry. As the season progresses into cooler weather, excess or unused sugar is stored.

Another distinction can be made about sweetness in vegetables. Bitterness in lettuce (another cold-hardy crop) also occurs when it has been stressed by heat, and as an annual plant, it goes to seed soon thereafter. Once it becomes bitter, it can never become sweet again because it's an annual. On the other hand, many brassicas and root crops are biannuals that won't produce seeds until the second season. This means that their sugar content can ebb and flow according to the needs of the plant. That's why there's such a wide difference in taste between hardy veggies of the same variety in different seasons.

Munching on the leaves of Austrian winter peas, a hardy cover crop that also tastes great

It's little wonder that the tender taste buds of children find initial introductions to cold-hardy veggies a memorably bad experience. But the fact remains that hardy vegetables have significantly more vitamins and minerals in them than summer crops, and a quickly acquired taste is possible if vegetables are harvested when they should be. I've found the easiest way to get kids to overcome their aversion to hardy veggies is to present the food raw. My kids ate raw broccoli stalk (peeled and sliced), carrots, turnips, spinach, and tender baby kale long before they ate those foods cooked.

It occurs to me that this whole issue of vegetable bigotry is only a matter of poor communication skills. Maybe we don't demand excellence in our grocery stores, so we receive products that look fine, but are inferior because of poorly timed harvest schedules. Perhaps we're psychologically trapped by childhood memories that scream out, "Warning! Warning! Warning!" whenever we think about voyaging into the realm of nightmarish adolescent culinary experiences. Who knows? At least it's food for thought the next time you stroll through the vegetable section at the local grocery store.

The One-Two Punch of Cold-Weather Gardening Empowerment

While you can learn a lot from books and by asking questions of other gardeners, there's only one way you can really become familiar with the various plants (and varieties of each) that are available that will perform well in your cold-weather garden. I call this method my "one-two punch," and you begin by taking the time to carefully read several seed catalogs. Order three or four catalogs and read the description of every variety of cold-hardy plant you're interested in growing, and pay special attention when it mentions specific varieties that "resist cold," are "hardy," "grow well in garden structures," or somehow indicate their appropriateness for cold-weather gardens. Read the sections of your catalogs that discuss those veggies and become familiar with the vari-

A fall harvest of salsify about to be enjoyed

ety names. Catalogs are a great source of information on cultivation and harvest, and you can vastly accelerate your knowledge of cold-hardy crops in a couple evenings of reading.

The second part of this process is to pick up a used copy of *Rodale's Encyclopedia of Organic Gardening* at your local bookstore. Look up every vegetable that you're reading about in the catalogs. I have three different editions, and the one I use the most is a comprehensive 1959 edition I swiped from my father's bookshelf many years ago. Though it is dated in regards to variety descriptions, it has told me everything I need to know about cold-hardy veggies and has been an invaluable companion.

You'll find this one-two punch will empower you with information beyond anything else that you can read.

Now before you grow veggies that you've never tasted, it's a good idea to try them out first. A good source is to go to your local food cooperative or local produce center. Most food co-ops sell fresh produce grown by local farmers, which means that in the winter, the shelves will be stocked with cold-hardy veggies. The local grocery outlet isn't likely to carry the more obscure greens that I'll talk about, but many co-ops will. It's an excellent opportunity to try out mustards and various salad greens. It's also a good opportunity to connect with folks who grow the food. People who work the veggie sections at co-ops are often familiar enough with their product to know variety names, and it's a good way to find out how other folks serve hardy vegetables.

The Cold-Hardy Veggies

As I've said, this isn't an encyclopedic survey of every hardy veggie ever grown, but simply a basic introduction to many of the hardy veggies that'll produce for you in the garden.

LETTUCE

The first crop folks usually raise in enhanced growing environments is lettuce, because it's easy to grow, and salad greens are enjoyed often by a large percentage of the population. I spend a lot of time on lettuce here because I get more questions about growing lettuce than any other crop. There are so many lettuce varieties to choose from, and the varieties sold in grocery stores are often so unremarkable. There are five types of lettuce.

Crisphead

The best-known member of this group is *Iceberg* lettuce. I've never grown this type, which was the most common lettuce available in the local grocery store where my mother shopped. My dad never grew lettuce—perhaps because he assumed that it all must taste as unremarkable as the slabs of *Iceberg* that frequented our dinner table, topped with mom's homemade ketchup/mayonnaise dressing. By all accounts of gardeners I know, it's hard to grow, low in nutritional value, and it bolts easily in hot weather. Still, it remains in seed catalogs, so somebody must be growing it—but why, I can't imagine. Not all crispheads are of the Iceberg type. Pat Battle, the head organic gardener at Highland Lake Inn in Hendersonville, North Carolina, can't say enough about an extremely heat-resistant and very sweet type of crisphead called *Bronze Mignonette*.

Looseleaf

These are the easiest to grow and last the longest in hot weather. Most cultivars have loose, open growth habits ranging from the tall and open (such as *Deer Tongue*) to the loose and frilly (such as *Lolla Rossa*). The classic American heirloom of this type is *Black-Seeded Simpson*. Other great varieties include *Green Ice, Oak Leaf, Salad Bowl, Grand Rapids,* and *Red Sails*. Battle raves about the distinctive taste of *Tango*, which he says may be his choice for all-time-best lettuce, even though it doesn't tolerate heat well. *Tango's* more vigorous root system makes it absolutely shine in cold weather. It also volunteers well and is excep-

Lettuce and claytonia

tionally well suited to cut-and-come-again harvesting. (Most looseleaf varieties will continue producing if you harvest the outer leaves as they grow, or will grow again if you cut them 1 inch [2.5 cm] above the ground.)

Butterheads

Butterheads aren't heat-tolerant, but they do well in cold weather. Their buttery texture makes them a favorite in our kitchen. Barry Rubenstein, an organic market gardener, produces thousands of lettuce plants each year. One of his favorites is a beautiful red butterhead called *Carmona*. I've had great success with Sangria, Buttercrunch, and Tom Thumb. Battle speaks highly of Nancy. Boston and Bibb are two lettuce varieties seen often in grocery stores. The great flavor of *Marvel of Four Seasons* and *Brune d'Hiver* made them as popular a century ago as they are today.

Romaine

Also referred to as cos, this is the most nutritious of all types (with high levels of vitamins A and B). It's easy to grow and very tasty. *Winter Density* is one of my favorite romaines (though it also has characteristics of a butterhead). Rubenstein reports that *Medallion* has excellent disease resistance and holds up well in the field. *Parris Island* is an old favorite among American gardeners. These lettuces take 70 to 85 days to mature, depending on the variety. A quicker-growing variety is *Little Gem*, which is smaller in stature.

Batavian

These large, upright, crisp, looseleafed lettuces taste great and can be harvested a leaf at a time. They also stand the heat very well. Rubenstein speaks highly of *Sierra* (as do other professional growers) because it withstands heat and tastes great. I've been impressed with the heat resistance and taste of *Anuenue* and *Victoria*, both of which will take the cold of late spring and still produce well into the summer.

Mesclin Mix

This is a high-priced combination of various baby lettuces and greens that's even finding its way into mainstream grocery chains. My first experience with mesclin mix, years ago, started when I spent too much money on a packet of "Gourmet Mesclin Mix." It was a bunch of lettuce cultivars mixed together. The instructions directed me to broadcast the seeds and they would all come up, allowing me to snip leaves at my leisure. Things didn't work out as I'd imagined, however. The different varieties matured at various times—nothing came up together. I had weeds coming up because of the lapse in time between the emergence of the various cultivars. In the end, in order to beat the weeds, I had to transplant healthy-looking, individual plants from the mix into other parts of the garden and dismantle the patch. If you want to grow mesclin mix, buy half a dozen varieties and broadcast the seeds separately in small plots, so each variety comes up on its own. Cut the baby leaves from each patch with a pair of scissors in the weeks after they emerge, and mix the harvest together.

Final Musings on Lettuce

There's really no all-around-best lettuce, because the numerous cultivars can be grown in such a broad range of temperatures and climates. The way to have a high-performance, lettuce-producing garden that has a great diversity of color and texture is to keep a dozen varieties in their packets in a sealed jar in the back of the refrigerator. I keep several packages of *desiccant* (they come in medicine bottles) with the seed packs to absorb moisture that might damage seeds. Stored properly, seeds will remain viable for a couple of years. And if you choose to, it's easy to save lettuce seeds to replenish your stash. As I add packets of various varieties to my stash, I write such cryptic messages on the packet as "heat tolerant," "extremely hardy," and "fall" or "spring," so I can grab seasonally appropriate packets when I want to plant newly recommended varieties that I haven't grown enough to know. This storage method will give you lettuce varieties adapted to a broad range of growing temperatures so you can sow a pinch of seed every couple of weeks—pleasing your palate and decorating your garden throughout the year.

OTHER ANNUAL VEGGIES

Archaeologists tell us that long before ancient native people were cultivating corn, beans, and squash in the mid-Atlantic and Ohio Valley states, they were selecting and growing a commonly occurring weed called lambs quarters. I still pick wild lambs quarters for my spring salads and wild-greens pesto, but there are a couple varieties available that have been selected for their large leaves and lovely purple edges. It's an example of weeds that have been domesticated once again, and are becoming steadfast winter crops. Another example, dandelion, was selected for its large leaves and milder taste. *Good King Henry* and *Orach* are two more wild greens that are hardy and are found in cold-weather gardens. You can get these in at least a couple of different varieties, they are all easy to grow, and they self-seed readily.

Spinach

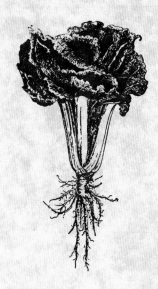

There are three other cold-hardy crops that produce terrific-tasting greens. Unlike lettuce, spinach can be sown thickly and you'll find that winter-grown crops have more succulent leaves. Just as there are turnip varieties that have been bred for their tops, so, too, are there beet varieties that have been developed to produce vigorous and very tasty green leaves. Swiss chard, a member of the beet family, is a cold-hardy crop that also survives summer heat very well. Chard is a cut-and-come-again green; if you cut it off 1 inch (2.5 cm) above the ground, it will grow again for another harvest, and it'll continue doing this until it goes to seed in the second year.

Corn salad, also known as "mache," is a crop that grew wild in Europe and was selected to grow in medieval gardens. It's a very mild-tasting green. While it's slow to germinate and is a small rosette when mature, it's very hardy and will self-seed if allowed to. It tastes great cooked or raw, and balances out the taste of stronger greens.

Carrots, salsify, and turnips are all root crops that are cold hardy and will continue growing well into winter.

The Austrian winter pea is a traditional cold-hardy cover crop that produces a healthy amount of biomass and releases a lot of nitrogen into the soil when it's turned under in the spring. It also tastes wonderful. Each winter, my kids love to graze on the slightly pea-flavored tops right from the garden. The tops taste great in salads and are a killer addition to winter pesto mixes.

Some Thoughts on Kale

As it turns out, even though my experience with kale resembles that of the kid at the beginning of this chapter who had to eat his veggies, no matter how poorly they tasted, kale has probably become my favorite green. In the cool weather of fall, we can eat kale anytime. In the summer, it's eaten only after we've had a few days of cooler and overcast weather. When leaves are harvested at the correct time, it's great sautéed and layered into a lasagna. It also makes a great winter pesto (see page 134), and it's simply elegant when lightly steamed.

Like the wild form still found in northern Europe, the many varieties of kale all have an upright and open-leafed habit that allows gardeners to cut off succulent leaves and then come again to harvest leaves many times more.

Though it doesn't take up much space, kale is a primary crop in my garden. It gets seeded directly as soon as the ground warms up in the spring, and I harvest leaves until the weather gets hot. Fifteen to eighteen plants give my family of four all the kale we need, and we're able to share plenty with our neighbors. In hot weather, I periodically prune off the overgrown and cabbage-

Red Russian kale

moth-caterpillar-chewed outer leaves to give vigor to the new and tasty leaves, which continually sprout. In the late summer, I again cut back outer leaves, and give my plants a side dressing of organic fertilizer or compost. The plants then give me a new burst of growth throughout the fall. A layer of floater fabric gives them enough protection to keep producing outside until early winter when they stop growing because of the cold.

They also perform well under tunnels or a greenhouse all winter, especially if I also keep them covered with floaters. Come early spring, these plants give me a fresh crop of leaves before they go to seed. Just before the yellow flowers appear, the kale produces little broccoli-like flowerets that are delicious. By the time last year's crop is gone, the newly planted spring crop is kicking in.

In cool weather, it's impossible for me to pass my row of kale without grazing on the tender leaves. They taste great and are packed with calcium, Vitamin C, and Vitamin A. I can't say enough good things about kale.

Red Russian has been our favorite variety for a number of years, but there's no question that aphids will attack a crop of Red Russian, leaving *Dutch Curled* or *Siberian* alone in the same row. I love the oblong crinkly leaves of *Lactiva* (also called *Dinosaur* by some of the local organic farmers in my region), but it isn't terribly resistant to aphids either.

THE REST OF THE BRASSICA FAMILY

Most folks are familiar with the more prominent hardy members of the brassica folk: cabbage, kale, Brussels sprouts, broccoli, cauliflower, and Chinese cabbage. But there's a whole mess of other lesser-known, but equally great-tasting, brassica. The leafy members of this tribe are arugula, collards, cress, mustard, rape, turnip greens, tyfon, and watercress. Besides broccoli and cauliflower, brassicas with edible stems and flower buds include kohlrabi, sea kale, and turnips.

THE COMPOSITE FAMILY

The chicories come from the *Compositae* tribe and have gained favor in the last decade as fancy restaurants have been using them in salads, soups, and main dishes. The four types of chicory are endive, escarole, radicchio, and witloof, and they all have a slightly bitter taste, which mellows when cooked, and adds zing to salads.

PERENNIAL VEGGIES

Perennial vegetable crops can be covered with some sort of contraption to force them, and there's a long tradition of folks doing this commercially to get higher prices at the market. By virtue of their nature though, they're crops that already thrive in cold weather. My chives, asparagus, and sorrel are up and edible in the early spring while I'm still pampering other cool season crops under the protection of contraptions. Especially if you're prone to stretches of time when you are busy elsewhere, you can't help but love a plant that comes up with a minimum amount of coaxing. I included perennials here because for the year-round gardener, these are crops that fill out a garden quickly.

Asparagus

Asparagus has a long tradition as a perennial crop that was forced by market gardeners inside movable cold frames that were set up over asparagus beds in early winter.

Though an established bed of asparagus will produce dependably for 20 years and more, it takes some work to get it started. And the commitment you must make with asparagus is the understanding that you can't harvest this crop for the first two years that it's in a permanent bed. And for a year after that, you can only harvest for four weeks to ensure that the plants are well established.

For many years, the old standby variety of asparagus has been *Mary Washington*. Like *Jersey Giant* and *Waltham Washington*, it's resistant to a disease called "rust." There are new varieties that have been developed to resist Fusarium wilt. It's worthwhile for you to find out what varieties are favored in your region before making your selection.

Sorrel

Sorrel is another perennial that should be in every hardy garden. It has lemony-tart leaves with a definite bite that mellows in cool weather. Sorrel is high in oxalic acid, and some recipe books suggest using it sparingly as flavoring in soups and sauces. But once you start eating this easy-to-grow perennial, you'll stop using the word "sparingly." Young and tender leaves taste great in the garden and in salad mixes. I like to add five or six of the big succulent leaves to sandwiches to add zest to my lunch.

When adding sorrel to the garden, look for the better-tasting French sorrel. Though it can be grown easily from seeds, you aren't likely to find it on the seed rack of your local garden center. But call around, and you'll often find a nursery or garden center that sells it as a potted plant. If the variety is questionable at the garden center, order seeds. It should be planted in an area where it can expand. As it grows, you can divide it and spread it out to make a small bed in the corner of your garden. When it goes to seed in the spring, cut it back to the base and you'll get a fresh flush of tasty leaves soon after.

Horseradish

Horseradish has had a longtime reputation as a medicinal. Poultices made from the grated root have been applied externally to relieve aching joints, and the juice has been taken internally for bronchial complaints since Roman times. A horseradish tea is said to be very effective against fungal and mildew problems. (Steep two handfuls of chopped leaves in 2 pints [.95 L] of water for 48 hours, strain, and dilute to four parts water to one part tea.) But the bottom-line reason to grow horse-radish is that there's no question that homemade horseradish is incomparable when slathered onto a bagel with cream cheese.

Horseradish, however, does have the tendency to take over a garden. The important thing is to dig up the horseradish bed each fall to harvest the roots. When the bed is clear of roots, cut off the rootlets from the main roots and replant the largest of those in vertical holes in the same bed you just vacated, burying the tops 3 inches (7.6 cm) below the surface and 12 inches (30.5 cm) apart. Soak the bed, give it a top dressing of compost and mulch, and leave it alone for another year. In spite of this knowledge, my patch of horseradish is well away from anything I love and is contained by mowing the grass sur-rounding it. It seems happy restrained in this manner, and I don't need to worry about it turning into a marauding monster if I miss a few roots.

Jerusalem Artichokes

Though neither native to Jerusalem nor an artichoke, this member of the sun-flower family has a long tradition in Native American gardens and reputedly kept hunger at bay when all else failed in the gardens of early pioneers. You'll find this root crop occasionally at your local co-op, and once you recognize it, you'll see patches of these tall plants along the edges of the gardens of old-timers in your area.

Though some consider the taste bland, others, like me, find it somewhat sweet and nutty. It's completely starchless and is often recommended to diabet-ics as a substitute for carbohydrates.

This virtually disease-free plant is aggressive and should be kept in a place where you can keep it isolated. I've seen patches that are planted specifically to create tall screens or windbreaks. Improved varieties have been developed for better flavor, and it's worth checking out catalogs to find newer varieties rather than plant roots of a vintage variety from the old-timer down the road.

The Possibilities of Pesto

I'VE MENTIONED PESTO several times in relation to cold-hardy veggies. Here's my method for making a great cold-hardy vegetable pesto (I don't follow a recipe, but I do pay close attention to ratios and procedure):

§ I like to use one green as a base and add another green to it at a rate of four to one to get a taste that kicks. Typical combinations are kale and mustard greens, spinach and sorrel, or spinach and beet greens. A lot of it depends on what's in the garden.

§ Add 5 parts greens to 1 part nuts and 3 cloves of garlic. Mix them all in a food processor. Add 2 parts grated cheese to the mix until it's a puree. Add 2 to 3 parts of oil slowly as the processor is running.

Chives, beet and turnip greens, sorrel, and mustard all give a terrific zing to pesto, but lettuce has too much water. Austrian winter pea shoots can be harvested with a pair of scissors to give the pesto a nice mild pea flavor. I've made pesto using cashews, walnuts, pistachios, and of course pine nuts, and they're all excellent. Sunflower seeds are really inexpensive, and their taste is very comparable when used in place of pine nuts. I've also found that mixing only 1 part oil makes a thicker pesto puree, which tastes great on bagels, or spread on peanut butter sandwiches.

Plant Hardiness Zone Map

Refer to this USDA map to determine your plant hardiness zone. This shows the lowest temperatures that can be expected each year in the United States and Canada.

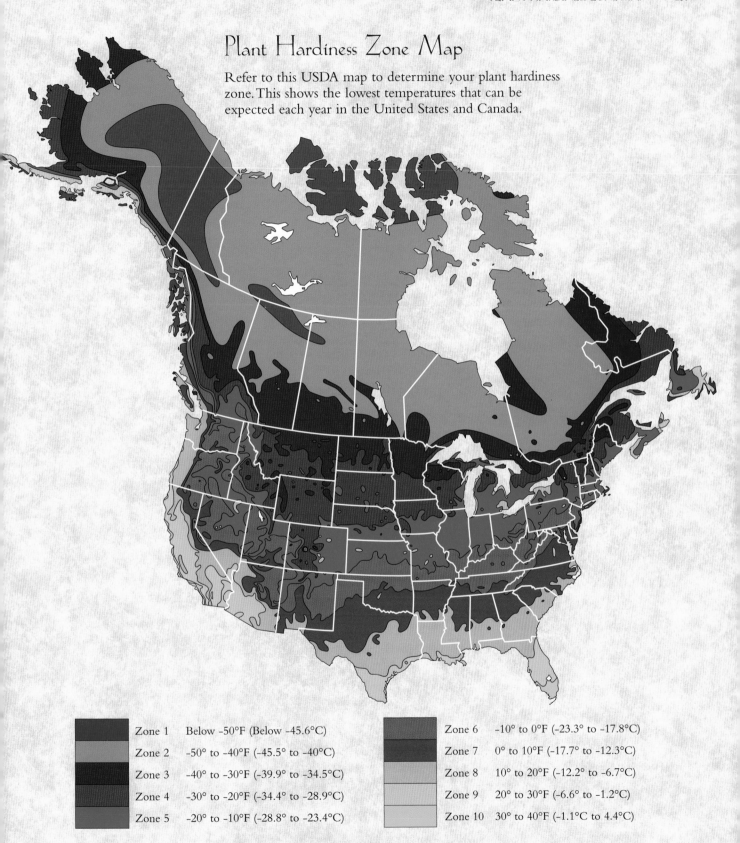

Zone 1	Below −50°F (Below −45.6°C)
Zone 2	−50° to −40°F (−45.5° to −40°C)
Zone 3	−40° to −30°F (−39.9° to −34.5°C)
Zone 4	−30° to −20°F (−34.4° to −28.9°C)
Zone 5	−20° to −10°F (−28.8° to −23.4°C)

Zone 6	−10° to 0°F (−23.3° to −17.8°C)
Zone 7	0° to 10°F (−17.7° to −12.3°C)
Zone 8	10° to 20°F (−12.2° to −6.7°C)
Zone 9	20° to 30°F (−6.6° to −1.2°C)
Zone 10	30° to 40°F (−1.1°C to 4.4°C)

Index